A word about the Toastmasters

D1079842

Who needs another book on public speaking, let alone a series of them? After all, this is a skill best learned by practice and "just doing it," you say.

True, but insight from people who've already been where you are might help ease some bumps along the road and provide handy advice on handling stagefright and knotty speech assignments.

After all, if practice is the best solution to public speaking excellence, why is this country so full of speakers who can't speak effectively? Consider politicians, business executives, sales professionals, teachers, and clerics who often fail to reach their audience because they make elementary mistakes, such as speaking too fast or too long, failing to prepare adequately, and forgetting to analyze their audiences.

Too often, we assume that because we try so hard to communicate, people will automatically understand us. Nothing could be further from the truth! Listeners will judge us by what they think we said, rather than what was intended or even said. Simply put, the meaning of our message—and our credibility—is determined by the reaction we get from other people. The purpose of *The Essence of Public Speaking Series*, then, is to help you in the communication process, prepare you for the unexpected, warn you of the pitfalls, and, as a result, ensure that the message you want to give is indeed the same one people hear.

This series represents the accumulated wisdom of experts in various speech-related fields. The books are written by academically trained professionals who have spent decades writing and delivering speeches, as well as training others. The series covers the spectrum of speaking scenarios: writing for the ear, using storytelling and humor, customizing particular topics for various audiences, motivating people to action, using technology for presentations, and other important topics.

Whether you are an inexperienced or seasoned public speaker, *The Essence of Public Speaking Series* belongs on your bookshelf. Because no matter how good you are, there is always room for improvement. The key to becoming a more effective speaker is in your hands: Do you have the self-discipline to put into practice the techniques and advice outlined in these books?

I honestly believe that every person who truly wants to become a confident and eloquent public speaker can become one. Success or failure in this area solely depends on attitude. There is no such thing as a "hopeless case." So, if you want to enhance your personal and professional progress, I urge you to become a better public speaker by doing two things:

- Read these books.
- Get on your feet and practice what you've learned.

Terrence J. McCann
Executive Director, Toastmasters International

. . . and from the National Speakers Association

For the true professional, school is never out. *The Essence of Public Speaking Series* was developed to share ideas and information with those who desire to accelerate their development as speakers. As a community of more than 3,700 men and women dedicated to advancing the art and value of experts who speak professionally, the National Speakers Association (NSA) welcomes this comprehensive educational resource.

A broad spectrum of talented individuals make up the field of professional speaking: consultants, trainers, educators, humorists, industry specialists, authors, and many more. NSA brings this wide variety of professional speakers together to better serve their clients, advance their careers, and help them reach a higher level of personal and professional development.

Throughout *The Essence of Public Speaking Series,* you will hear the voices of NSA members offering their expertise and experiences. This sharing of ideas and knowledge is a key element of NSA membership. NSA's founder and Chairperson Emeritus Cavett Robert said, "Experience is the only thing that's worth more secondhand than first-hand. We don't live long enough to learn through trial and error, so it's best to get your O.P.E. degree—Other People's Experience."

The "information age" is creating a huge demand for professional speakers. The fact that education is one of the top growth industries in the world should come as no surprise. What may seem surprising, however, is the fact that when we're speaking of education, we are not referring to the traditional colleges and universities. Instead, it is the learning that is conducted daily in the hotels and corporate training facilities. The "faculty" for these learning experiences are often professional speakers.

Speakers are a key element in the growing meetings business. The American Society of Association Executives reports that the meeting market is a $75 billion industry. Moreover, the American Society for Training and Development estimates that well over $100 billion is expended annually in the field of human resource development alone.

The audiences of the new millennium will be different from the audiences of the past. They are not content to sit and be passive listeners; they want to take an active role in their own learning; and require cutting-edge information presented in a technologically savvy manner. The speakers and trainers who fail to deliver the information and content these audiences can utilize immediately will notice that audiences are not afraid to vote with their feet.

So, we welcome you to the world of speaking. As you read the volumes in this series, you will explore many facets of public and professional speaking. You are about to embark on an important learning experience—one that will broaden your vision as a public speaker and perhaps instill a desire to make speaking an important dimension of your career. NSA, the "Voice of the Speaking Profession," stands ready to provide you with information on the speaking industry and the resources you need to make a speaking career a viable option.

Edward E. Scannell, CSP, CMP
Interim Executive Vice President
National Speakers Association

"Alan M. Perlman's book could have been entitled The Ultimate Speaker's Manual. *It is filled with technical suggestions, practical counsel, and tools that any speaker can use immediately."*

> — Russ Johnston, DTM, Toastmasters International Accredited Speaker, real estate developer, and agriculture's number 1 motivational stand-up comedian

"In a style that is easy to read, Alan Perlman clearly outlines the tips and techniques for writing winning speeches . . . every time! This book is a must-read for every speaker."

> — Mark Brown, ATM, Toastmasters International 1995 World Champion of Public Speaking, Senior Systems Analyst, The Reader's Digest Association, Inc.

"Alan Perlman's fresh, practical insight into such speech basics as purpose, audience, structure, and style should prove alike helpful to a student, an instructor, and the speaker struggling to put together a talk for next week. Perlman's extensive examples from his experience as a professional speechwriter prove that he practices what he teaches. His chapter on ceremonial speeches is worth the price of the book."

> — Jerry Tarver, author of *The Corporate Speechwriter's Handbook*

WRITING GREAT SPEECHES

Professional Techniques You Can Use

ALAN M. PERLMAN

WILLIAM D. THOMPSON
Series Editor

ALLYN AND BACON

Boston   London   Toronto   Sydney   Tokyo   Singapore

ISBN 0-205-27300-9

Printed in the United States of America
10 9 8 7 6 5 4 3 2 1   02 01 00 99 98 97

To my mother,
and in memory of my father,
with love and thanks
for teaching me
the importance of learning
and the power of words.

Contents

Preface

WHAT ARE "PROFESSIONAL TECHNIQUES"?

One of the world's most overrated fears is the fear of giving a speech. According to a survey (which appeared in *The Book of Lists*[1] but which nobody seems able to document) speech giving is the most anxiety-producing experience of all, surpassing bugs, heights, sickness, and even death. "I'd Rather Die Than Give a Speech" proclaims the title of a recent book.[2]

Oh, really?

If I held a gun to your head and gave you the choice, I'd think you'd pick the speech. After all, what's the worst that could happen? You'd appear foolish, shallow, inappropriate, inarticulate, insensitive, ill-informed, or all of the above. None of those is as bad as dying.

On the other hand, they're all pretty serious. There are good reasons why performers speak metaphorically of "dying" onstage. Your image and reputation are important, and you want public speaking to enhance—not destroy—them.

I should know. I write speeches for a living. I put words in the mouths of corporate executives—words that they agree to say because those words reflect either their ideas, or the ideas of the organization we work for, or ideas of my own that are compatible with both.

I do this successfully, year after year, despite my lack of a business degree, management experience, or formal training in almost every subject I write about. In the high-pressure, no-mistakes world of executive rhetoric, I manage to keep both my job security and my speakers' reputations from suffering untimely demises. I avoid death by speechifying, and I can show you how to do the same. I take care of the CEO's image—and I can show you how to take care of yours.

Why? Because the basic components of every speech situation are the same—a speaker, an audience, and the desire of the former to influence the latter's thoughts, beliefs, or behavior via the use of words. So whether you're a student of speech communication, an aspiring professional speaker, or a businessperson, politician, educator, or Toastmaster who wants to upgrade his or her skills, some or all of the challenges I face will be familiar to you, and many, if not most, of the skills I've developed belong in your professional toolkit. Let me run down the specific and demanding requirements that a professional speech/ghostwriter must fulfill, and you'll see what I mean.

1. **Understanding the audience.** I need to know as much as possible (or to make educated guesses) about the people who will hear the speech—their expectations, their background knowledge, their attitudes toward the speaker and his/her topic.

2. **Creativity on cue.** It's not enough just to talk about a subject. I must do so in a new and interesting manner that rouses listeners' emotions or connects with their concerns. I must help audiences to see the subject in a different and perhaps unfamiliar way. I must give the speaker a variety of novel approaches to the same material.

3. **Instant expertise.** I know precious little about most of the subjects I write about, but to create an effective speech, I must come up with 10 to 30 minutes' worth of relevant material, at a level of sophistication equivalent to that of speaker and audience.

4. **Familiarity with relevant and peripheral trends and with Big Ideas/mega-themes.** A speech is generally not about one thing; it's about many things, and it's about the relationship among them. Every speech must address the "so what?" factor. It must establish the relevance of its subject matter to the listeners' lives and world. So I have

to understand what's going on in the world outside the speech. I have to identify key ideas and relate them to each other, to the audience's concerns, and, if possible, to some larger theme.

5. **Support of points and arguments.** They won't believe it unless I help them believe it, with convincing facts, examples, citations, and quotations.

6. **Creating memorable "curtain up/down" openings and closings.** These are the most important parts of the speech, sometimes the only ones the audience remembers. A speaker can't just start talking. He/she has to warm up the listeners, get them used to his/her voice and speaking style, and prepare them for what is to come. Similarly, ending with, "Well, that's all I have to say," is completely unacceptable. Where's the crescendo that tells them it's over and leaves them inspired, informed, committed, or in some other desired state?

7. **Meeting inflexible deadlines.** I have to do 1 through 6 now, because the speaker is waiting for his/her draft. For me, there are no "late papers." Speech dates, once set, almost never change. This is not a profession for procrastinators.

8. **Conformity to rigid time/length specs.** This is necessary because most speeches are part of a larger program. Or because the speaker's—or audience's—time is limited. Or the speech-form has its own requirements (e.g., about two to seven minutes for welcoming remarks). Or, given the speaker's skills and the "grab factor" of his/her subject matter, we simply want to stop before we tax the audience's patience or attention span. I have to be able to control length so that the speech, when presented, fits exactly into the prescribed time limit.

9. **Speech coaching that ensures the best possible delivery.** Not all corporate clients want it, but those who do want it expect it to make a difference.

Those are some of the professional techniques that enable the ghostwriter to survive and thrive. There are others—such as profiling and reproducing the client's individual style—that are peculiar to the ghostwriting profession. But the ones I've just outlined are the most relevant to you if you're going to write your own speeches. And by the time you finish this book, you'll understand them and be able to apply them to your next speech-writing task.

Sound interesting? Great! Then let's get on with it.

NOTES

1. David Wallechinsky, Irving Wallace, and Amy Wallace (New York: Bantam Books, 1977), p. 469.
2. Michael Klepper (Irwin Professional Publishing, 1995).

1 Deciding What to Say

I am convinced that all writers are optimists, whether they concede the point or not. How otherwise could any human being sit down to a pile of blank sheets and decide to write, say, two hundred thousand words on a given theme?

Thomas Costain

How indeed? You don't have to have a two-hundred-thousand-word writing task to know what Costain is talking about. Many people are stopped cold by the challenge of writing a memo to the boss, a progress report to the Finance Committee, or a one-page article for the church newsletter, not to mention a full-length speech.

Part of the problem is that they don't know what the speech should say. This chapter shows you how to decide.

PURPOSE CONTROLS CONTENT

Maybe you already have some or all of the content of your speech, in the form of "topics I want to discuss" or "points I want to make." Or maybe all you have is a subject, and you have to develop the content from scratch. Whichever it is, you begin by asking the first of several questions that will lead you to your subject matter itself, namely, **"What's my purpose?"**

This is a key question underlying all communication. You are asking, *"What am I trying to accomplish by composing and delivering this particular message to this particular audience?"*

You want to move your audience from Point A (where they are—intellectually, emotionally, or behaviorally—before you start speaking) to Point B (where they are afterward). So what's Point B? What's the change you want to bring about by communicating? What are your listeners supposed to be thinking, feeling, believing, or getting ready to do when they've finished listening to you?

Purpose is a fundamental concept, because *the reason we communicate is to get things done—to bring about change in someone's thoughts or actions.* It was true a million years ago when our earliest ancestors shouted across the grassy plains to warn each other of an approaching hyena—and it's true today when a strategic planner delivers a presentation to convince senior management that the company should seek new distribution channels.

"Well," you may ask, "what about conveying information? Don't I make a speech in order to tell people things?"

Of course. But there's always some purpose behind your wanting your audience to know whatever it is that you're telling them (as opposed to anything else you could tell them). If there weren't, it wouldn't matter what you wrote. You might as well read them the phone book.

So **purpose controls content** means that your decisions as to what to write must be governed in part by whatever changes you seek to make in your listeners' minds, lives, or behaviors.

PURPOSE: NO SECRETS

There should be no secrets about your purpose. Your listener's must be able to understand all your intentions. They must understand why each piece of your speech was included and how it fits with the rest. They should never be left thinking, "Now why is he/she telling me this?"

HOW TO FOCUS ON PURPOSE

Strategy #1: Goal and Target

You can focus on your purpose by identifying your goal and your target. Your goal may be to **confirm**, **challenge**, or **change.** And your target may be the audience's **emotions**, **beliefs**, or **behavior.** You therefore have nine possibilities:

	Emotions	Beliefs	Behavior
Confirm	1	2	3
Challenge	4	5	6
Change	7	8	9

Let's look at what each of these purposes involves.

Purposes 1 through 3: You're soothing and complimenting the audience, assuring it that the way it feels about some issue, thing, or event is OK, that its beliefs are correct, that its conduct is appropriate.

If people are happy the way they are, is such communication redundant? Not necessarily. Your confirmation could be a part of—or a prelude to—some larger purpose. Or, because of your own importance, the audience may need to know that you share its beliefs (this freedom of important people to repeat the obvious is what I call "platitude latitude").

Purposes 4 through 6: Your purposes here are to upset your listeners' balance a little and to cause them to question their own attitudes, information, or actions.

With 4, challenging beliefs, you may be trying to reassure anxious people—or to unsettle complacent ones. With 5, you're presenting new information about accepted truths. With 6, you offer new solutions to old problems, new paths to traditional goals, or even new goals.

Purposes 7 through 9: These are the most ambitious of all. You seek change. You want people to actually get mad—or to calm down. You want them to really accept your view as their own. You want them to get up, go out, and behave differently.

Of course, you may have more than one purpose. And one of the nine may underlie and reinforce another, especially in the Change category; it's difficult to change behavior unless you attack the beliefs and feelings that underlie it. But the 3 × 3 scheme gives you a way to focus on just what you're trying to do.

Strategy #2: Labels

Another way to focus on your purpose is to find the right label for it.

Our language has a wealth of words that refer to communicative acts: *urge, persuade, convince, recommend, illustrate, demand, explain, inform, discuss, define, predict, (dis)agree, analyze, elaborate on* . . . and many others. Just pick the one(s) that will accurately label what you're trying to do. You can even use your label(s) in the opening of your speech, with a tail-end that expresses the substance of your purpose:

> I want to EXPLAIN **[tail-end:]** the evolution of our reporting systems, DESCRIBE **[tail-end:]** the difficulties of our present system, OFFER **[tail-end:]** solutions to the problems, and CONVINCE you **[tail-end:]** that my proposals are the best ones.

FROM PURPOSE TO CONTENT

Now you see how the notion **purpose controls content** can help you decide what to say. Everything that helps you accomplish your purpose(s) goes in. Everything that doesn't goes out.

You can use this system if you already have some of your content (in the form of, let's say, a list of ideas or points you want to discuss); focusing on your purpose(s) helps you decide what to keep and what not to. You can also use it even if you have no idea of what you're going to say, because when you know what you're trying to achieve, you know what kind of subject matter you're going to have to produce; you can identify the factual information, expert opinions, numerical data, quotes, citations, or whatever you need in order to successfully confirm, challenge, change, urge, discuss, or accomplish what you've set out to accomplish with this particular audience.

AUDIENCE CONTROLS CONTENT

What goes into your message is determined not only by your purpose but also by the needs of your audience.

In many speech situations, you have very little personal acquaintance with your audiences. And yet, if your communication is to be effective, you have to make some assumptions—otherwise, you'd be in the position of someone who had to buy a gift for a total stranger: you could certainly make the purchase—but you'd have no way of knowing how the recipient would react.

That's why you have to ask yourself the following questions. If you don't know your listeners well enough to answer them yourself (in general terms, of course; there will always be exceptions among the audience members), then you may need to talk to people in the organization to which they belong—or to people you know who will be in the audience. As you answer each question, add the necessary material to what you already have—or take it away, whichever is appropriate.

Audience/Content Question #1: Does my audience understand <u>why</u> you're delivering <u>this</u> message?

In other words, do they understand your motivation? Before you even open your mouth, will they already know what problem or background issue motivated you to communicate?

If the answer is yes, there's no problem. Many speaking assignments are carried out in an organizational context. Someone has asked you to research, evaluate, report, and so on. Audience/Content Question #1 has been answered even before you begin. But if the answer to Question #1 is no, be sure to explain your motivation (preferably near the beginning of your speech). For an example, see Chapter 3, Opening Strategy #2.

Audience/Content Question #2: How much background knowledge can I assume on the part of my audience?

The less background knowledge you can assume, the more explanatory information you must supply. That information falls into two categories:

1. **Explaining unfamiliar concepts and defining unfamiliar words.**

   Do some preliminary thinking about your talk or presentation. Will there be terms and concepts that your audience probably won't understand? Later on, read through your notes or script and answer the same question. Be sure to define each unfamiliar term or concept. For example:

   > We have to understand this value issue in all its subtleties, and that's going to be a challenge.

Value does not mean "price." Consumers calculate value by comparing "what I pay" against "what I get," where "what I get" is a <u>bundle</u> of features and benefits.

This may seem a little squishy, a little subjective, and indeed it is. Different economic groups of consumers calculate value in different ways. It's not just a matter of income. You might find this a little surprising, but it's the more educated, economically advantaged consumers who are leaders in some value-oriented behaviors.[1]

2. Supporting unfamiliar ideas.

Think through what you plan to say, and identify all the ideas and propositions that the audience might not accept as given. Do the same with your notes or finished script. If you find ideas and propositions that your audience may not accept, provide the reasoning that leads up to them—or the information that supports them (but give only as much as your audience needs—and no more).

This process can be tricky: underexplain, and you lose them; overexplain, and you bore them and turn them off. So give this question serious thought, and add or remove material accordingly. (Sometimes, if you think some audience members will understand but others won't, you'll need to hedge gracefully with "As you may be aware" . . . or some similar expression.)

In the following example, the speaker supports an unfamiliar idea—the need for his audience to change. He uses personal testimony ("what we did at <u>our</u> company") plus anecdotal material that explains how change is both necessary and exciting.

Let me turn now to the third key to success: **low-cost production.**

This one promises big payoffs for you. Meat industry data show large differences between low- and high-cost growout and processing operations . . . and turkey is similar to other meat sectors in this respect.

Cost-cutting is really your strong suit, and I urge every one of you, in your individual companies, to pursue it—aggressively. It's not easy, as I can tell you from personal experience. Kraft has taken some very tough steps to get to where we are today. Earlier this month, we concluded the sale of our plant in West Liberty, Iowa. We made this hard decision—to close the plant that Louis Rich built in 1943 and that had served as its headquarters since 1960—so that we could get closer to low-cost production.

Of course, it's not all pain and suffering. Everywhere in our company, people have come up with really creative ideas and productivity programs that have given us incredible cost savings in just a few years. And you can do the same.

You win by playing to your strength. When your industry is highly competitive and costs are volatile, you win by focusing on that part of the value chain where you're strongest.

I know this is a difficult, emotional issue for you . . . as it was—and still is—for us. But let me assure you that it is an absolutely essential component of your bridge to excellence. . . .

First off, and perhaps toughest of all: we all have to **acknowledge the need for change.** This is not an easy thing to do. They say that the only person who likes change is a wet baby, and that's probably not too far from the truth.

Managing change to your advantage also means **being acutely sensitive to your environment.** I've tried to help you this morning, with my comments on the consumer.

You know, there's an experiment in biology—you may have heard of it—where a frog is placed in water, and the temperature is slowly raised. And it's actually possible to do this so that the frog is boiled before it knows what's happening.

We all run the risk of getting cooked if we don't notice the small changes taking place . . . the subtle ways in which the future is taking shape right now, today, all around us.

Managing change means **looking critically at everything we do.** Long-established practices, procedures, and habits of mind are the most suspect. According to an old Japanese proverb, "If you sit on a stone for three years, you will get used to it." We have to be constantly asking ourselves, "What stones are we sitting on? What have we gotten used to?". . .

How do you know when to change? Here's some good advice from a writer named Frank Burgess: "If in the last few years you haven't discarded a major opinion or acquired a new one, check your pulse. You may be dead."

The future never just happens. It's created, sometimes by accident, usually by people acting consciously and seizing—and creating—opportunities. And that happens not when people resist change . . . but when they welcome it and manage it.

Lester Thurow, the Dean of MIT's Sloan School of Management, put it very succinctly; he said, "A competitive world has two possibilities for you. You can lose. Or, if you want to win, you can change."

There's one more piece to this business of managing change—in some ways, the most exciting of all.

In Greek mythology, there was a god named Proteus. He triumphed over all his challenges by changing his shape.

In the same way, when we respond to our challenges, we reinvent ourselves—and our companies. We change to become better, faster, smarter, stronger. Each success lays the foundation for the next one.

And it's this process that brings us the personal and professional satisfaction that we want . . . and makes our businesses every bit as profitable and successful as we want them to be.[2]

Audience/Content Question #3: Do my listeners already understand why my subject(s) and my conclusion(s) are important, interesting, or useful to them?

If you're not adding to their understanding of their world or fulfilling some other goal you know them to have, why should they pay attention at all? But you <u>are</u> enlightening them, and you may have to tell them how.

Maybe you're offering a new path to accepted goals. Or new conclusions from old assumptions. Or new interpretations of old facts. Or new facts.

Again, it's a strategic choice: if you can take for granted their need to know what you have to say, don't blow your own horn. But if they're not aware of the value of your contribution, you'll want to explain it (preferably at the beginning of your speech).

For an example, see Chapter 3, Opening Strategy #5.

Audience/Content Question #4: Is my audience adequately aware of my expertise or authority?

If you can assume that your audience regards you as qualified to speak on this subject, you can let it go at that. But if not, you may have to buttress your credibility, by referring to your

- background, training, and education;
- position within the organization;
- acquaintance with the available knowledge on the subject;
- first-hand experience; or
- contact with people who have any or all of the above.

Credibility is important. On the basis of your knowledge of your listeners, you'll have to decide just how much convincing they need. Here's an example:

> It's that time of year once again—time to kick off our 1996 United Way campaign.
> I'd just like to speak briefly about why I personally support United Way. I want to do that because, although we each have our own reasons, we also have some reasons in common.

What I'm about to tell you is based on 25 years of experience with United Way agencies, beginning when I was a junior marketing person at P&G.

Initially, I had the responsibility of helping to manage the campaign at a small Cincinnati company . . . then, over the years, I worked with bigger and bigger companies . . . and groups of companies and institutions . . . and I eventually served as a member of the New Agency Admissions Committee of the United Way Board.

Years later, when I was President of General Foods USA, I headed up the campaign right here in Westchester-Putnam Counties.

As General Campaign Chairman, I personally visited many United Way agencies. I also worked closely with the trustees and with the full time staff that administers United Way.

I saw first-hand what United Way agencies do for the community. I know what United Way dollars do—and how well they do it.

Now, out of all that experience come the reasons why I've always supported United Way as generously as I could.[3]

Audience/Content Question #5: To what extent do my listeners already agree with me?

This question is critical to your purpose, of course: You can't aspire to move your audience from Point A to Point B unless you know what their Point A is. You need to be aware of your audience's beliefs so that you don't make any unfounded assumptions.

Review your speech at each stage of preparation. Be aware that it's probably based on your view of how things are. If that's also your audience's view, fine. People are more attentive to ideas that they already accept, and they retain more of what they read or hear if the underlying assumptions are friendly and familiar.

On the other hand, if what you're planning to tell them is based on assumptions that they might not accept, go back and put in the facts, examples, personal experiences, or other data that will help them to think the way you do.

Similarly, if you're presenting a solution to a problem, be sure that your audience agrees that it is a problem. If your proposal will lead to certain results, make sure that these are results that your listeners also value.

Don't get caught short. Assess the gap between what you have to say and what your audience holds dear. If that gap is too wide, you must help the listener to cross it.

In the following example, the speaker explains why his proposals should not be perceived as threatening. He uses several strategies. In the fifth paragraph, he calls upon the authority of a famous author, who supports his view, although on a different but related subject. In the next paragraph, he points to examples, prefaced by a patriotic note. The eighth paragraph further diminishes threat by assuring the audience that nothing that it holds dear will change under the speaker's proposals. The speaker closes on a metaphoric, idealistic note that—very subtly—implies that the audience should be ashamed not to "look beyond [its] narrow interests" and share his lofty view.

> So there you have our common agenda: training a generation of managers and professionals who can quickly innovate, effectively communicate, and creatively merge the power of tomorrow's technology with the skill and dedication of tomorrow's workforce.
>
> And is academic freedom compromised in all of this? I really don't think so.
>
> I'm aware that some people think that academic freedom and practical applications are like oil and water—that professors must research and teach utterly without regard to the use that might be made of their findings and teachings . . . and certainly without regard

to whether they'll be doing American business any good.

Well, I question that point of view. I just don't see it in either-or, black-and-white terms. I think that it really is possible to pursue two apparently conflicting goals at the same time.

There shouldn't be anything so terribly shocking about that. It's kind of like the way F. Scott Fitzgerald defined *intelligence:* "the ability to hold two opposing ideas in the mind at the same time, and still retain the ability to function."

Indeed, this is one of America's great strengths. Politicians with differing points of view find their common ground, reconcile their conflicts, and go forward. In business we do that all the time. Labor relations in our industry is an excellent example. We have a strong tradition of adversarial unionism. And there are some things about that tradition that really aren't too helpful to our drive for higher productivity and lower cost—which, of course, are also in the union's interest. So our agendas agree in part, and they conflict in part. And we simply have to reduce the conflicts, cultivate the areas of agreement, and move ahead—together.

The same sort of progress has to go on between business and academia. We have to cooperate in ways that help businesses to contribute to the economic health of our society and allow academics to pursue free inquiry and expression of ideas.

And, of course, all I've done today is offer suggestions whose consequences seem to make sense from my—admittedly biased—perspective. It's still up to each individual instructor to decide what to teach . . . how to teach it . . . or just what the students will know and be able to do after the final exam is all over and the grades are all in.

One last thought: Adlai Stevenson once observed that the astronomers of the world cooperate partly because there is no one nation from which the entire sky can be seen. Perhaps we too must look beyond our narrow interests so that we too can see the entire sky.

And perhaps when we do, we'll be able to see that the stars of academic freedom and national competitiveness can indeed shine side by side, each illuminating—and neither diminishing—the other.

BOTTOM LINE: PURPOSE, AUDIENCE, CONTENT

I've just given you five key questions which, along with your purpose(s), will control your content. But don't stop thinking about purpose and audience after you do a first version of your message. Go back and ask the key questions again and again. **Measure your speech against the preconditions for its existence: speaker's purpose and audience's needs.** These serve the same function as the foundation of a building: you don't see it—but without it, you've got a very shaky structure indeed.

NOTES

1. "Building the Bridge to Excellence." Keynote remarks by Robert A. Eckert, Group Vice President, Kraft Foods, at the annual meeting of the National Turkey Federation, San Francisco, CA, Jan. 13, 1997. All the examples in this book are from speeches that I wrote.

2. Robert A. Eckert, *ibid.*

3. United Way Campaign Kickoff remarks by Robert S. Morrison, CEO, Kraft Foods, White Plains, NY, Oct. 2, 1996.

Sequence: Putting Things in Order

BACKGROUND: AN INTERESTING PARADOX

I know an executive who insists that he can't write anything until he can think of a title for his document. That's a recipe for writer's block—and it's not even necessary. The truth—paradoxical though it may seem—is that although communication is <u>received</u> in a linear sequence, it isn't always <u>composed</u> that way.

Sometimes you begin with your conclusion and fill in the steps that lead up to it. Other times you begin with a jumble of ideas that you'll develop into the middle of the document. And then there are the situations in which all you have to start with is a single idea—or just your purpose. In all of these cases, you create the rest according to the principles in the last chapter.

In this chapter I'll show you how to organize your material—and <u>then</u> put a suitable beginning and ending to it.

Your speech will be much more effective if you can learn to arrange material in the appropriate order—and convey that order to the audience. Why are these skills so critical? Because *the arrangement of your text—in other words, the relationship of your ideas to each other—is an important part of your message.*

HOW TO ORGANIZE: SEVEN PATTERNS

Let's begin with the material you've selected—essentially, the middle of your document, the heart of your message. This part must have some shape, some organizing principle, that corresponds to your purpose(s). You have seven basic possibilities; think of them as building blocks. Any one of them can provide the overall plan that accomplishes your purpose. Or you can use more than one.

We'll consider them one at a time. I'll describe each one in terms of your various "X"s, which are whatever you're talking about—things, concepts, people, events, statements, trends, processes, and so on.

Organizational Pattern #1: Description

You have one or more X's, and you accomplish your purpose by describing its (or their) parts, components, or characteristics.

Organizational Pattern #2: Relations

Three possibilities here. You accomplish your purpose by explaining

- how two or more X's are similar to or different from each other, or
- how one includes another, or
- how one is actually a part of another.

Organizational Pattern #3: Variation

You have one or more X's. To accomplish your purpose, you

- explain the different forms each one can take, or
- give various examples of each one.

Organizational Pattern #4: Sequence

Here you accomplish your purpose by putting two or more X's in order. You

- show how they have occurred in a particular historical or chronological sequence, or
- give the events (or processes) that furnish the background for other events (or processes).

Organizational Pattern #5: Cause/Effect

To accomplish your purpose, you show how

- one X results from one or more previous X's, or
- one causes another (or others).

Organizational Pattern #6: Consequences

You accomplish your purpose by projecting the effect(s) or implication(s) of or the outlook for one or more X's.

Organizational Pattern #7: Judgment

You accomplish your purpose by explaining why a particular X (or X's) is (are) good or bad, desirable or undesirable.

Use #1, #2, . . . or All Seven

Your organizational plan can include more than one of these. Once you describe the *relationships* between two X's, you might then need to discuss their *consequences*. You might then want to employ *judgment*—to tell the audience why these effects are desirable. It all depends on your purpose— that is, on your intended impact on your audience's thoughts, feelings, or behaviors.

HOW TO OUTLINE

Think of your outline as a "pre-speech." Creating an outline is a helpful way to see all the pieces of your text at a glance. It also shows you how each piece of your message is related to the others so that you can signal these relationships to the audience. In fact, making these relationships explicit is the biggest benefit of outlining, so be rigorous: ask yourself, over and over, questions such as "Is this really a subpoint—or is it the next main point?" and "Is this really a subpoint of this point—or does it belong somewhere else?"

Any of the above patterns can, by itself, be the basis of your outline. Or your outline can include two or more of them, plus an introduction and an ending. If this is the case, I suggest you include the name of the pattern—"Consequences," "Judgment," or whatever—when you write out each main topic so that you'll remember to help the audience follow the way you're developing your subject (see the next section).

By the way, don't use the Harvard outline system, with all its letters and Roman numerals—too hard to remember. Instead, use bullets, dashes, and other symbols to mark the parts and subparts of your text, so that you can move material around in your word processor and not be concerned about changes in numbering.

Two "Off-the-Shelf" Outline Plans

Some combinations of the seven patterns are used more frequently than others. Here are two that are very common in business and professional communications because they reflect the problem-solving and deliberative processes of business/professional people and their organizations.

1. PROBLEM ⇒ SOLUTION
- BACKGROUND (#5: CAUSES of problem or situation)
- PROBLEM (#1: DESCRIPTION)

- PROPOSED SOLUTION (that will give the desired EFFECTS [#5])
- CONSEQUENCES (#6; includes positive and/or negative consequences)
- ACTION (that's needed to achieve the CONSEQUENCES [#6]).

2. "BIO" (BACKGROUND-ISSUES-OUTLOOK)

- BACKGROUND (#4: what has happened, in chronological SEQUENCE, up to now)
- ISSUES (to be considered or decided—the EFFECT of what has gone before [#5])
- OUTLOOK (that is, the likely CONSEQUENCES [#6])

SEQUENCE: THE SPEECH AS STORY

Finally, regardless of the organizational pattern(s) you choose, you should try to impart some sort of "directional flow" or "forward thrust" to your message. Think of your speech as a story—and of yourself as storyteller. The parts of it that occur earlier in real life should occur earlier in the speech.[1] Thus, I would always talk about my "experiences" before I got into the "lessons learned," because that (unfortunately) is the way real life works.

HOW TO SIGNAL
YOUR ORGANIZATIONAL PLAN
TO YOUR AUDIENCE

Since your plan helps accomplish your purpose by putting ideas into the appropriate relationships, it is a key aspect of your message. So you must signal it to your listeners.

Here's how: for each of the seven plans, you use words that **announce** and **describe** what you're going to do (or are doing); then, within that particular plan, you use other words to **remind** the audience of what you're doing.

Here are some suggestions. Once you grasp the general
principle, you can supply others that may be better suited to
your particular message.

Organizational Pattern #1: Description
- Words that **announce/describe**: *discuss, describe, analyze*
  (e.g., "In this report, I will **analyze** the reasons for . . . ")
- Words that **remind**: *component, characteristic, element, facet,
  aspect* (e.g., "Another **element** of the problem is . . . ")

Organizational Pattern #2: Relations
- To **announce/describe**: *compare, contrast, differentiate*
- To **remind**: *is similar to/different from, includes, consists of,
  comprises*

Organizational Pattern #3: Variation
- To **announce/describe**: *explain the variations in, survey the
  different forms of, give examples of*
- To **remind**: *varies, is an example of, for example, for
  instance, exemplifies, (also) appears as, takes the form of*

Organizational Pattern #4: Sequence
- To **announce/describe**: *trace, review, recap(itulate)*
- To **remind**: *precedes, follows, by way of background, then,
  later, next, subsequently, after that*

Organizational Pattern #5: Cause/Effect
- To **announce/describe**: *explain, account for*
- To **remind**: *reason, cause, factor, result, effect, impact*

Organizational Pattern #6: Consequences
- To **announce/describe**: *predict, project, forecast*
- To **remind**: *implication, benefit, pitfall, outlook, consequence*

Organizational Pattern #7: Judgment
- To **announce/describe**: *assess, evaluate, judge*
- To **remind**: *(un)favorable, (un)desirable, (un)acceptable,
  (in)appropriate* (e.g., "Another reason why this proposal is
  unacceptable . . . ")

NOTE

1. Of course, these can be reversed for special effect, as when a speaker presents conclusions first, then gives the reasoning that led up to them, or describes some bright vision of the future, then talks about what we'll have to do to get there. But I hear too many amateur speeches that are just an incoherent jumble of ideas, which is why I encourage you first—before you try for special effects—to learn to put your ideas in a natural, free-flowing order.

3 Beginning and Ending Your Speech

Now that you know what your message is, you're ready to put a beginning and ending to it. It may seem strange to discuss beginnings and endings <u>after</u> we've talked about the body of the speech. But to me, this is the only approach that makes sense: how do you know how to introduce and end the speech when you don't know what it's going to be about?

HOW TO BEGIN: THE FIRST WORDS OUT OF YOUR MOUTH

You <u>could</u> plunge in with a stunning, mind-grabbing quote, story, or statistic. This gambit may work, but it's risky. People often don't like to have their attention seized; they prefer to have it coaxed out of them (remember, you're a storyteller). And you'd be taking a chance that your grabber, uttered amidst the clanking of coffee cups and the rustle of bodies getting settled in their seats, wouldn't grab.

I have no problem with opening with some variation of "Thank you for inviting me. It's great to be here." You might also talk briefly about your interest in or experience with your listeners' organization or their cause. Or you might thank them for taking time out of their busy schedules (if that is indeed the case), or for attending despite the heat, cold, rain, or snow (which might itself merit some light comment).

Trite? Sure! But so are "Take care" and "Have a good one."

In a world where so much is unpredictable, predictability has its place—in this case, as a "channel-opener" that gets your listeners used to your voice and speaking style. And the subject should be one that you and your listeners share first-hand knowledge of and that requires little or no intellectual effort to discuss—namely, the situation at hand, the speech-event and the conditions surrounding it.

Once you've opened the channel in this way, you can proceed to your attention-getting gambit—a stunning statistic, perhaps, or an amusing anecdote, or a provocative question or quote—that in turn leads into your opening strategy. (But don't feel that you have to use any of these gimmicks—you can also go right from your channel-opener to your opening strategy).

FIRST WORDS: BEHAVIORAL BONERS

As you prepare to deliver those all-important first words, I must warn you against the following violations of etiquette:

- **Complaining about anything.** That includes travel hassles, food, drink, lights, mike, size of room (anything having to do with the set-up should have been checked, but if something does go wrong, you must have the grace to rise above it). No tapping on the mike. No asking, "Is this thing on?" It had better be, and that's all there is to it.

- **Gratuitous and/or protracted humor.** Many people think a speech should begin with humor, but the fact is that you are not there as an entertainer. So refrain from telling your favorite joke unless it is hilarious, G-rated, and relevant. Similarly, the audience is not interested in a long, meandering account of what happened to you just the other day or on the way over here. No matter how amusing it seems to you, skip it, unless you're sure it will be genuinely funny to your listeners (you might field-test with an audience member or two) and relevant to the audience, occasion, and speech topic.

- **In-jokes.** Once you're up there, it <u>is</u> OK to greet or recognize important individuals who are present—for instance, officials of the organization or of the government, or dignitaries or celebrities of some sort. But <u>no</u> private conversations, from the podium, with good ol' Charlie at the head table, and <u>no</u> oblique references to what happened at the bar last night. Excluding people is bad manners.

- **Disavowals of public-speaking ability.** There's nothing I know of that turns an audience off more effectively than "Well, I'm not much of a speaker, so here goes nothing!" If you're not so hot, they'll figure it out for themselves soon enough. Just do the best job possible with the skills you have—and skip the disclaimers.

- **Tactless response to the introduction.** Don't belittle it or suggest that it was too flowery (even if it was) by saying something like "After that introduction, I can hardly wait to hear what I'm going to say" or "I never knew I was that interesting." Responses like these, even though you'll find them in speaker's handbooks, make you sound arrogant. Remember, you're an invited guest. The last thing you want to do is to antagonize the program chairman, the introducer, or the audience in the first few moments of the speech.

- **Negative references to the speech.** Don't say anything about how long or boring it may be or how it may tax the audience's attention span. Again, you'll find such openers in the speaker's handbooks (e.g., "I'm here to speak, and you're here to listen. If you finish before I do, please let me know."). No matter how much openers like these make you chortle in the privacy of your office, don't use them. Even if you do get a laugh, it comes at the price of making your listeners length-conscious, right at the outset. And who needs that?

And please, no opening anecdotes about long-winded speakers. Never suggest that your speech will be anything but brief and interesting (as indeed you have tried to make it). If it's not, the audience will figure that out for themselves.

■ **Abandoning your prepared support and "speaking from the heart."** Deciding to wing it is appropriate about one time in one thousand. If you want some idea of when it is appropriate, look at the catastrophes listed in your homeowner's insurance policy: nuclear war, act of God, and so on. Point: Unless circumstances change so radically that a whole different speech is called for, this cliché is a recipe for disaster.

HOW TO BEGIN: FIFTEEN STRATEGIES

Once you're past the introductory amenities, you need some way to get into the body of your speech. Here are some possibilities. Your purposes and your audience's needs will help you decide which one(s) to use.

Opening Strategy #1: Give a summary of what follows. For example:

I just want to chat informally for a few minutes and offer some observations on the state of our business in general and on our minority dealer activities in particular.

Opening Strategy #2: Explain your motivation for communicating (if the audience doesn't know it).

I want to express my enthusiastic support for your organization and its goals. In our interdependent world economy, nothing could be of greater value to the peoples of our two nations than to promote open, two-way trade. Corporations benefit as well, because no single company has all the good ideas.

That's why we've formed business partnerships with three different Japanese companies.

But my main focus this morning is in the other direction. I want to help you with one of your goals—to promote the policies and interests of American business in Japan—by telling you a little about what we've done, in our industry in general and at our company in particular, to build products that are worthy of export to Japan . . . and in fact to any country in which we do business.

Opening Strategy #3: Comment on your relationship to or experience with the audience or the subject, especially as it relates to Opening Strategy #2.

It's a great pleasure to be part of this event. First, I'm delighted to offer my personal tribute to your new Hall of Famers.

I remember what James B. Conant, the former president of Harvard, once said: "Each honest calling, each walk of life has its own elite, its own aristocracy based on excellence of performance." Well, we in the business fraternity are no exception. We have our elite . . . our finest examples of achievement, leadership, and integrity . . . and I'm pleased to recognize the inductees that we're honoring tonight. I respect all they stand for . . . I admire all that they've accomplished . . . and I'm proud to be associated with them.

Now, the other reason why I'm so enthusiastic about being your speaker tonight . . . is that I'm a whole-hearted supporter of better economic education in this country. We've heard a lot lately about how Americans need to brush up on geography . . . that too many of them can't even find their own country—let alone the Persian Gulf—on a map. Somebody's even decided that Americans don't know enough about everything in general! So he published a "Dictionary of Cultural Literacy"—just to set down a common base of knowledge. Well, I think economics deserves just as much attention as any other field, and I'm glad to see an organized effort in support of it.

Opening Strategy #4: State your purpose— or the hoped-for outcome of your remarks.

1. Tonight I want to contribute to the mutual understanding of business and academe. I want to help bring down the wall that some people say stands between us. And I want to influence the education of tomorrow's marketers, so that they'll be better equipped to cope with the realities that they will very soon be facing.

2. My intention today is to give you an overview of the career possibilities that are available here, so that you can get a clearer idea of just how these fit in with your ambitions.

3. I have a wealth of news and information for you this evening. And when I'm done, I expect—at least I hope—that you'll have a clearer understanding of where our company is headed in this intensely competitive and swiftly changing industry of ours . . . as well as some insight into the plans, programs, and products that we believe will help maintain our position as a leader in that industry.

Opening Strategy #5: Describe what's new, interesting, useful, or beneficial in what you're about to communicate (if the audience isn't aware of it).

> My purpose here today is to take a good hard look at—
> to reevaluate, reinterpret, maybe even rediscover, in a
> sense—something that's always been one of our key suc-
> cess criteria: speed to market.
>   Those of you who know me will remember that I've
> always pushed to get things done quickly. But really, the
> ideal of getting there faster is no stranger to any of us.
> We all know that in any business, if consumer demand is
> there, you have to be fast enough to meet it—or you
> could lose out in a big way.
>   Another thing we know is that the pursuit of speed to
> market can inspire new creativity and discipline in the
> organization.
>   With today's intense global competition and rapid
> technology transfer, it's obvious that speed to market is
> more important than ever.
>   But speed alone doesn't guarantee success . . . and
> faster isn't better when you miss the mark. All of which
> brings me to the question I'd like to consider today. We
> must constantly look for ways to do things faster.
>   But since the fastest car doesn't always win the race,
> what does it take to win?

Opening Strategy #6: Describe the background or context for what you're about to say.

This description could take the form of a narrative or personal experience. In the following example, the audience's
familiarity with the subject was itself the background for the
talk, so the speech begins with a "non-introduction":

> I'm pleased to have this opportunity to offer a few
> thoughts on a subject that's of intense and immediate
> interest to all of us in American industry—and that I
> personally feel very strongly about, too.

You've heard of speakers who supposedly "need no introduction." Well, this is a speech that needs no introduction. I don't want to open with a joke or funny story, because our subject is anything but humorous. And I don't want to start off with alarming statistics that grab the audience's attention and awaken them to the fact that there's a problem.

You already know how drug use in the workplace is a reflection of what's going on in society at large. You already know how seriously drugs undermine the health of employees who abuse them. And you already know the impact of drug abuse, not only on the safety and morale of everyone else in that work environment, but also on the quality of the product—and thus on the competitiveness of the business.

So . . . instead of "introducing" my subject in any of the standard ways, let me just begin with three simple principles that I think must be the starting-point for any corporation that's serious about a drug-free workplace.

Opening Strategy #7: State the overall plan of your speech—that is, describe the way you've organized your subject matter.

As I look back at the progress we've made, and at our prospects for the future, I'd like to offer some thoughts on a single broad question: how can we most effectively take advantage of this enormous and encouraging potential? And here I have three answers—which I'll present in the form of three challenges.

First, a challenge to our entire industry: As we develop tomorrow's products, we must devote particular attention to the public concerns that are now emerging and that show every sign of continuing over the long term.

Second, a challenge to each individual company: To make sure that within its own operations, the potential of electronics to enhance every aspect of the product's ownership and operation is realized quickly and at the lowest cost.

And third, a challenge to you engineers as individuals and professionals: To cultivate the attitudes, strategies, and approaches to professional development that will ensure that you participate as fully as possible in the exciting times that lie ahead for your firms and for our industry as a whole.[1]

Opening Strategy #8: Give an example (or examples) of what you're writing or talking about.

Many magazine and newspaper feature articles begin in this way. Here's how I employed the technique in one of my own speeches (the subject was Pat Buchanan's rhetoric):

> For some of us speechwriters—especially, I would say, those of us in politics—speechwriting is not a lifetime activity but a way station in a career.
>
> William Safire, who wrote for Nixon, branched out in two directions, becoming an opinion peddler and a popular language expert.
>
> Peggy Noonan went on to use her White House experience and Washington connections to market herself as a sage commentator on politics and everything else.
>
> Dana Rohrabacher, who also used to write for Reagan, is a Congressman, and James Fallows, a speechwriter for Jimmy Carter, has made himself a respectable living as a journalist, beginning with a book, *The Passionless Presidency,* that was (and here I'm quoting from a column in Monday's *Trib*) "a long attack on the personal failings of Jimmy Carter." Bad boy! Our relationships with our clients are confidential and should not be for sale.
>
> And then we have Patrick J. Buchanan, another former Nixon scribe. Pat is supposedly a congenial, but in reality a very angry man who inflames passions he

can't control and proposes solutions that not only won't work, but—if Pat should ever gain the White House—promise massive increases in government power, on the way to a theocratic America that sounds like something out of *The Handmaid's Tale.*[2]

Opening Strategy #9: Play off a current event or idea, either agreeing or disagreeing with it.

The first of the following two examples disagrees; the second agrees.

1. The last time I spoke here was in 1985. Since then, a lot has gone on in the world.

I remember a Doonesbury cartoon from last year that had Howard Baker reporting to President Reagan that capitalism was making such tremendous progress—and communism suffering such setbacks—all over the world that the Cold War was over—and we had won! The last panel of the cartoon showed joyous mobs in Times Square, waving their newspapers and pointing their index fingers to the sky in the familiar gesture that says "We're number 1."

Well, as so often happens, yesterday's amusing cartoon idea is today's serious academic proposition. Since 1985, not only has the Cold War ended, but so—supposedly—has history itself.

That's according to a recent paper by a State Department planner. He said that there would be no more vast conflicts between ideological systems. Liberal democracy with capitalist economics has proven to be the best system we can devise—the final form of human society. So all we have to do now is adjust, fine-tune, and improve.

Well, I think that any movement to a political and economic system that provides opportunity and rewards innovation and initiative has to be better—just for the sake of human dignity, let alone prosperity.

But I'm not about to start gloating.

As many critics of the "we're number 1" position are quick to point out, we still have plenty of work to do. In the world at large, there's still too much suffering to allow the slightest hint of complacency. And for us in business and industry, there's a long and formidable "to-do" list; no one who thinks seriously about it for one minute is going to be up for popping champagne bottles over the supposed "victory" of capitalism.

To begin with, there are the perennial tasks: to lower our costs and respond to our customers' needs . . .

In addition to our competitive agenda, we also have a social agenda . . .

2. Today we're honoring leading-edge agencies, whose work we enthusiastically support . . . and who, along with companies like mine, are defining what the future of interactive advertising will look like.

Of course, we can't know the future; if we could, it wouldn't be the future. But you can get a strong hint of the direction in which interactive will develop . . . by reading the cover story of the December 16 issue of *Time* magazine. It's called "Finding God on the Web," and it's subtitled "Across the Internet, believers are examining their ideas of faith, religion and spirituality."

The article says, in part,

> Almost overnight, the electronic community of the Internet has come to resemble a high-speed spiritual bazaar, where thousands of the faithful—and equal numbers of the faithless—meet and debate and swap ideas about things many of us had long since stopped discussing in public, like our faith and religious beliefs. It's an astonishing act of technological and intellectual mainstreaming that is changing the character of the Internet and could even change our ideas about God.

I found this article fascinating! Whatever your religious beliefs, it is truly an amazing example of how rapidly—and precisely—the Internet can respond to well-defined needs of consumers . . . and how it can even change the ideas that are being communicated. More than ever, the watchword of our times is, "The Internet is the answer. What is the question?" In other words, the Internet can literally be all things to all people. So what is it that people need it to be? It is this issue—and not the technology *per se*—that should be the focus of both companies like mine . . . and agencies like yours.[3]

Opening Strategy #10: Begin with a general—but related—subject and connect it to the audience and the speech-topic.

This example presents a tantalizing view of the future, followed by a transition to the audience's concerns.

> I think your choice of a theme is right on the money. The only way we can address tomorrow's needs is to take advantage of today's opportunities. That's exactly the mindset we have in business. If we didn't prepare for the future by acting in the present . . . we'd probably never get anywhere!
>
> And I'm very grateful for the invitation to come down here and talk to you this evening . . . because you've given me a rare chance to help make something happen in an area that I care very deeply about.
>
> As I was thinking about what I'd say to you this evening, I picked up the current issue of one of the popular-science magazines. It's a special issue, devoted almost entirely to the dawn of the 21st century. The year 2001 is only 13 years away. And what does the future hold?
>
> Well, if the experts in the magazine are correct—and they're just basing their predictions on projects already underway at academic and corporate research centers—we'll have robots with artificial intelligence . . . robots that can operate independently of human control—to do household chores, work in coal mines, or explore other planets. We'll live in plastic homes with a single

master control panel that runs everything from the stereo to the security system. We'll have home computers that have no keyboards because they'll be able to read our handwriting and understand our speech . . . and we'll be able to store entire libraries in a device that's no bigger than a slim volume of poetry.

We'll have digital musical instruments that don't even exist today . . . automated medical diagnosis and treatment . . . cotton that comes out of a test tube . . . new body parts created from our own flesh . . . cars that are fully controlled by electronics and that can even sense obstacles the driver can't see . . . and—this is my favorite—artificial sugar and fat that taste exactly like the real things, but have no calories whatsoever!

Yes, it's going to be a great new world, vastly different from today. But after I put the magazine down, I got to thinking. What about our society? After all, the relationship between technological and social progress is not strictly one of cause and effect. So what will the future hold for us? Will we all arrive at the 21st century together? Will all—or even most—of us be able to avail ourselves of this technological abundance? Or will we be even further polarized into a nation of haves and have-nots?

The answer lies partly in the hands of the people in this room—and of thousands upon thousands like you, all across our nation. There is perhaps no issue, with the exception of world peace, that is more worthy of our attention and our energies.

I have no doubt that everything the technology prophets foretell will, in one way or another, indeed come to pass. Technology has its own natural momentum, created by scientific curiosity (people asking, "Can we do this?") and by market forces (people asking, "Can we sell it?"). But the driving force for philanthropy must constantly be renewed. It begins with the altruism of families, organizations, and individuals like yourselves, unselfishly devoted to the welfare of other human beings.

Nowadays it seems that we're rowing upstream, not only against the natural currents of indifference and the "I've-got-mine" mentality . . . but also against a *number* of external realities that make our task that much more difficult.

Opening Strategy #11: Talk about the audience itself—its feelings, beliefs, attitudes, situation, accomplishments, or challenges.

1. I'm going to follow what I believe is the first rule of public speaking: know your audience. I've tried to imagine what's going on in your heads, and to do that, I recalled what was going on in mine when I graduated. On the basis of that, let me make a few guesses. I'd say it's a complicated mix of thoughts and emotions.

You're probably feeling elated and exhilarated today. You've made it over a very high hurdle. But you're apprehensive too, because many more hurdles lie ahead, some of them even higher than this one.

You also feel secure and accepted. You've formed strong friendships here, some of which may last the rest of your lives. But you're a little sad too, because you'll have to say some goodbyes today, and the truth of it is that many of the people who have shared your college experience will play a much smaller role—or perhaps no role at all—in your lives from now on.

And you feel educated and prepared. You've just put in four tough years acquiring both knowledge and ideals, and you're ready to put them all to work. But you're a little anxious, too . . . because if there's one thing that you've learned from this excellent institution, it is that your education has barely begun.

In fact, I'll go even further: in the complex, rapidly changing world that lies beyond this beautiful and serene campus, the substance of what you've learned has already started to become obsolete! But don't let that worry you too much. It's really the qualities of mind that count—so much so that one writer defined "education" as "what remains after we have forgotten all that we have been taught."

And as for your ideals . . . I hope you're concerned about them. You should be—because, as you may already be aware, they're about to be put to a severe test in that world you're about to enter.

I'm reminded of Bob Hope's classic advice to graduates. Having warned them about the "cold, hard world" that lay ahead, Hope offered two words of wise counsel: "Don't go."

But eventually, of course, you have to go. And that brings me to the questions I'd like to consider today: What are you likely to find when you get there, and how do you keep your ideals burning bright, despite the fact that, time after time, the real world seems to throw cold water on them?

2. Good evening, everyone, and let me say right off what a pleasure it is to be back once again with some of my favorite people—electrical engineers.

I think it's important to get together and talk with you every now and then, just because we're living in a time of such rapid and exciting change. The guy who said you can never step into the same river twice—because the constant flow makes it a different river—ought to be around today to see what we've got: a swift and powerful current, with lots of twists and turns, and plenty of white water. But I think it's great—and so should you . . . because it all creates, if you'll pardon the expression, a whole raft of new challenges for engineers. And through it all, your work is the same—and yet different, too.

It's the same in that the engineer's role is still to turn innovative ideas into real products—into elegant, simple solutions—that work, that improve people's lives . . . and, because they do all this, that help the organization win in the marketplace.

But your work is different, too . . . because you must do all of this under rapidly changing and often trying conditions which—and here's the good news—

give you new outlets for your creativity and new opportunities for you to contribute to the success of the whole business.

Let me give you a quick rundown of what those conditions are.

Opening strategy #12: Begin with a vision, which the audience will have a hand in realizing.

It's a pleasure to be here at a conference of such a key group of our company's leaders. And it's an honor to sound the keynote for this gathering. The keynote I'd like to sound this morning—the phrase that symbolizes what this conference is all about—is . . . PLAN TO WIN. Today we'll be presenting an important part of our Plan to Win—and we sure as heck plan to win with it.

Think for a minute about what it means to win. Imagine products that are so good—so on-target and loaded with value—that customers can't get enough of them. Imagine us passing the competition and racking up market share with one great product after another. Imagine the trade press going wild over our latest innovation. Imagine our service technician vying with the Maytag repairman for the title of "loneliest guy in the world." And imagine—really fix this one in your mind—us the undisputed Number One in the industry. Imagine the pride of our people . . . the admiration of the press and the public . . . and the envy of the competition.

It <u>can happen</u>. And today we're going to talk about some powerful new tools that will <u>help</u> make it happen.

Opening Strategy #13: Play off the title of the program, the theme of the conference, or the letter of invitation.

1. I happened to get a look at the postcard that gave notice of the meeting of your Association—you know,

the one that begins with the words, "With so much uncertainty in the industry . . . "

Well, that kind of got me to thinking. Yes, we do have to deal with uncertainty. But even more challenging are the certainties of our business:

- the certainty that competition will continue to intensify . . .
- the certainty that product lead-times will get shorter . . .
- the certainty that everything about our business . . . will continue to change . . .
- the certainty that government will have more and more to say about the kind of products we build . . . and . . .
- the certainty that creativity . . . will help decide who's going to be the winner in the marketplace of the '90s.[4]

2. I thought I might take a few minutes this morning to help you build your bridge to excellence. I don't know much about architecture, but it seems that one thing you need to do early on . . . is to **understand the environment, the terrain, the lay of the land.**

To me, that means the marketplace . . . especially the key factor in that marketplace—the consumer. The consumer is the judge of whether we're excellent or not. The consumer is the final arbiter of whether we're providing real value. So first, a few comments on what we know about the consumers of the late 20th—and soon to be 21st—century.

Then I'll talk a little about **the strategies that will get that bridge built** . . . with an emphasis on adding consumer value . . . and a special focus on advertising, which I know you're about to get into.

Finally, a few thoughts on what you might call the **"intangibles" of successful bridge building: the motivation, the drive, the spirit and mindset** with which you and I need to confront challenge and change.[5]

Opening Strategy #14: Talk about the organization.

Compare or contrast it with similar organizations or with
other organizations that go by the same name.

> Thank you and good afternoon. It's a real pleasure
> to address what I understand is the largest non-Greek
> student organization on the University of Michigan
> campus.
>   And yet, as I was on my way over here, it occurred
> to me that the differences between you and those
> other groups need not be that significant. "Michigan
> Economic Society" translates rather easily into "Mu
> Epsilon Sigma"—or "Mu Eps" for short. From there,
> the rest flows quite naturally: a secret handshake
> (moving the clasped hands in a wave motion to
> simulate the business cycle) . . . an initiation ritual
> (in which the inductee must recite a passage from
> Adam Smith backwards) . . . and, of course, regular
> meetings in a private "Malthus Room" in which a
> midday meal would be served at a charge of, let's say,
> a dollar, thus symbolizing the fact that there is no
> free lunch.
>   Moving beyond the superficial, though, I do think
> that we economists really are something of a fraternity.
> We have three chapters—academic, business, and gov-
> ernment—and the members of each must function
> under different conditions, although, having served
> time in all of them, I can tell you that business and
> government are more similar to each other than either
> is to academe.
>   Another sense in which we're a fraternity is that
> what we do is sometimes misunderstood, and not only
> by the layman but also often by the executives and
> politicians with whom we work directly. Anyone who
> doubts that has merely to witness the plethora of
> economist jokes, of which I will spare you even a sin-
> gle example.

Opening Strategy #15: Play off the date, day, month, or year.

What happened on this date in history? In this year? What else is this month devoted to?

> Welcome, everyone. I'm glad you could make it, because it's going to be a very interesting morning . . . and I think very much worth your while.
>
> We're here today to kick off an important new momentum-building initiative—Kraft Foods' first-ever Supplier Diversity Month.
>
> Now, out there in the rest of the world, a lot of groups have already laid claim to October. It's Healthy Lung Month . . . it's National Crime Prevention Month . . . it's National Liver Awareness Month . . . it's National Pizza Month . . . it's National Pasta Month . . . it's Vegetarian Awareness Month . . . it's National Clock Month . . . it's even Auto Battery Safety Month—and that's only a partial list. But we're not going to let any of that distract us from our focus, all throughout October and in the months ahead, on <u>supplier diversity</u>.
>
> Why this new focus? And why now? Those are the questions I want to answer in the next few minutes. I also want to talk about you. What are the challenges of supplier diversity? And—equally important—what are the rewards?[6]

HOW TO END: SIX STRATEGIES

When you have given the audience enough material to accomplish your purpose(s)—just enough and no more—it's time to end. But typically, you can't just stop, any more than you can walk away from a conversation without saying good-bye. There has to be a little leave-taking ritual, something to give the audience a sense of closure and resolution.

Here are six broad closing strategies. Each can be shaped to fit your audience and occasion. And each can be expanded via itemization (e.g, in #1, your message may mean <u>four</u> different things; in #2, you want them to take <u>three</u> different actions). Also, if it's appropriate, consider closing by saying something nice to or about the audience, as in the first example.

Closing Strategy #1: Net

Sum it all up, with emphasis on what your message means for your listeners, or for their world, or for the world that you both share.

> In the last few minutes, I've taken a look at the future of the industry. And here, in a nutshell, is what I see: new levels of quality, reliability, and maintainability . . . improved efficiency . . . and lower life-cycle costs—all made possible by standardized specs and advanced technology, especially microelectronics. The upfront investment may be higher, but the overall reductions in the cost of operation will be worth it.
>
> And it's our challenge as manufacturers to <u>make</u> it worth it—to give you the optimal trade-off, through innovative design, automated manufacture, and—most important of all—continued communication with your organization.
>
> On that note, I thank you for the opportunity to participate in your conference. I especially want to congratulate you and your organization for the way you're contributing to the progress of our industry. And I wish each of you every success in taking advantage of the many exciting opportunities that lie ahead.

Closing Strategy #2: Action/Commitment

Explain what action you hope your listeners will take as a result of having absorbed your message (<u>optional</u>: restate your purpose first), as in the first example, or on their own, as in the second. You might also close by explaining what action you

hope some other entity—your organization, Congress, etc.—
will take, on the basis of the facts, information, and arguments
you've presented. Or make a personal commitment or pledge
on behalf of your organization, as in the third example.

1. Let me now return to my keynote: action. In the next
two days and in the weeks ahead, what actions might
follow from the ideas I've presented?
    First, I think that we should try to give those stu-
dents who aspire to business careers . . . the guidance
that will allow them to make the most of their humanities training. And that means making sure that they
understand the similarities between humanistic and
business values, as I've been discussing them.
    To accomplish this, colleges and universities could
hold mini-conferences, panels, seminars, workshops,
or short courses, well publicized and offered to students and faculty alike. . . .
    Action Item #2 has to do with the differences in
outlook that I described. Corporate human-resources
professionals and the college placement counselors
must become more aware of these differences, so that
they can help job applicants find suitable and reward-
ing places in business. . . .
    Finally, I have some actions that I'd like this group
to take. . . . I'd like each of you to make one contact
from the other side of the fence, and plan to see that
person in the next few weeks, specifically to imple-
ment the ideas that you discuss in the next two days.

2. I hope this program will help you to grow in knowledge and sophistication . . . and make you more aware
of the strategies for success in our rapidly changing
global marketplace. But there is one more component—
a critical component—of your development as a business manager and leader, and this one you must work
on yourselves.
    I am referring to your growth as a person. There's a
Yugoslav proverb (and since I'm from Bulgaria, that's

close enough) . . . and it goes like this: "If you wish to know what a man is—place him in authority."

That proverb applies directly to your career: your growth in personal stature must proceed along with your growth in corporate status . . . so that you approach each new position as a more fully developed human being.

And here is my suggestion for planning your personal growth: "Become the person you would like to promote."

Continually ask yourselves what you would look for in such a person. Intelligence, dedication, hard work—certainly. But we should also include honesty, integrity, sensitivity to the needs and dignity of other people—qualities of not only the good manager, but of the good life as well.

I'm sure you can add to my list. In fact, I encourage you to do so . . . to keep your own list and measure yourself against it. Set personal goals, just as you set goals for your business unit. And work conscientiously to meet them. In this way, you will fulfill the requirements for becoming an outstanding manager, as well as a real human being—and a true citizen of the world.

3. Let me conclude with one simple thought: We see our agenda for the 1990s very clearly and are committed to pursuing it.

That agenda contains two key items; both of them are enormously important. The first is to continue to excite and satisfy our customers in every way. And the second is to address, wholeheartedly and energetically—and in fact to take a leadership position on—the social and public-policy issues in which our industry and our products are involved.

I pledge that our company will continue to lead the way toward these two goals. I ask all of my colleagues in our industry worldwide . . . to join me in this commitment. That is our obligation, not only to our own future, but also to the societies around the

world that grant us the right to exist and do business.
For them, we can certainly do no less.

Closing Strategy #3: Outcome/Outlook

Explain what is likely to happen (or what you hope will happen) as a consequence of your proposals or of the conditions
you describe in your speech (<u>optional</u>: restate your purpose first).

1. Let me close by observing that our industry has been
called a "hinge on the door of the economy"—a hinge
between the smokestack industries that have con-
tributed so mightily to this nation's prosperity in the
past . . . and the high-tech industries that hold so much
promise for its future.
　　If that's true—and I believe it is—then we can play
a pivotal role in the renewal of America's economic
health, vigor, and competitiveness.
　　And that is a role that we are fully prepared to play.
　　You can't turn the clock back. But you can wind it
up again. And that is what we <u>must</u> do . . . <u>can</u> do . . .
and <u>will</u> do. We've begun our comeback, and we know
how to sustain it. I'm optimistic that this early success
will give us the determination to go forward . . . to
make America the competitive giant that it once
was . . . and ultimately to hand over the reins of this
enormously productive and powerful nation to the
economic leaders of tomorrow.
　　Nothing would give me greater pleasure.

2. I believe that the European Union will develop into a
dynamic, unified market—a new and vigorous player on
the world economic stage. And I look forward—as I
hope <u>you</u> do—to seeing the dream become a reality.

This strategy can also be executed by means of rhetorical
questions—to which the answer is always an obvious and
emphatic YES. Here's an example:

Yes, these are astonishing times, full of hope and change. Can we rise to the occasion? Can we match the achievements of those around us—and indeed, our own achievements of the past—with new responses to the challenges we face? Can we carry our spirit of partnership and cooperation forward . . . and create a purchase and ownership experience that brings total satisfaction to the customers of the 1990s and the 21st century?

I say that we can . . . we must . . . and we will.

Closing Strategy #4: Confirmation

Restate your purpose (e.g., "I hope I've convinced you that . . . "; "I hope you now feel that . . . ").

Someone once observed that the future is where we will spend the rest of our lives, so we had better be aware of it. If I've increased your awareness in some small way, then our time together has been well spent.

This is a variation of a formula you can adapt to your own speeches: "I'm convinced that [state main premise of your speech]. If I've convinced you as well, then our time together has been well spent."

Closing Strategy #5: Qualities

Close with the qualities, talents, or attitudes that the audience (or some larger entity—the organization, the nation, society, or even humanity as a whole) will need in order to accomplish the goals or realize the ideas you've laid out.

Let me close on an optimistic note.

One of the great strengths of our system is its capacity for what's been called "creative destruction": the tearing down of what's no longer useful, as a prelude to building something better in its place.

Smart technology . . . smart public policies—we
can have both. But we'll need to reach deep into the
pocket of our national treasure.

I'm not talking about money, important as that is.
I'm talking about our real wealth: our American inge-
nuity . . . our zest for teamwork and hard work . . . our
capacity for risk and renewal.

They've never let us down before. Nor will they
now.

Closing Strategy #6: Bonding

Describe the way(s) in which your message reinforces (or
establishes) the ties that bind you to your audience, or the
audience members to each other or to some larger entity.

One last thought: our company's challenges are worth
discussing because they're not peculiar to us . . . They're
all over American business and industry.

Some firms have made great progress; others, not
so great. But I don't think the process ever ends.

Every organization has to be in close and constant
touch with its customers so that its products reflect customers' tastes, preferences, and expectations. Every
organization has to be working to involve every individual, directly and actively, in the success of the enter-
prise . . . and to promote the personal and vocational
fulfillment of all of its people. And every organization
has to be relentlessly searching, within and outside, for
new ways to cut lead times, exploit technology, and
innovate faster.

For the more we nurture innovation, the more we
become what Peter Drucker calls "an entrepreneurial
society [in which] innovation and entrepreneurship
are normal, steady, and continuous" . . . where they
are "integral, life-sustaining activities."

Such a society need never fear the future. It is creating it, every day.

POWERFUL ENDINGS: THE LAST WORDS OUT OF YOUR MOUTH

Regardless of which strategy you choose, always try for a final "crescendo," so that—just as with the end of a musical performance—the audience is left in a heightened emotional state and with a satisfying sense of closure. To do this, you must focus on all aspects of the ending.

- **Content:** Make the ending the "highest'" part of the speech—in breadth, view, ideals, and concept (relative to the rest of the speech, of course: the ending of a business presentation such as a quarterly sales report should be a little higher than the rest—but soaring rhetoric would be out of place).
- **Phraseology:** Use strong, vivid, concrete, specific words.
- **Rhythm:** The last sentence should have several strong word-accents, one of which should fall on the last word. Also, groups of three statements or concepts fall more strongly on the ear and mind than do two or four (as with the three repetitions of "every organization . . . " in the last example).
- **Climax:** The speech should end with either a long sentence that builds suspense or a long sentence plus a short sentence that finishes the thought in a mind-catching way.

All of the examples above fulfill these criteria. Read each aloud. Notice the use of rhyme (*teamwork* and *hard work*), alliteration (*risk* and *renewal*), and rhythm (e.g., the four strong beats on *Nor will they now.*).

You can build all of these factors into your endings, but you'll have to work on them. For maximal impact, consider scripting out and memorizing your ending (even if you're speaking from notes), so that you can look right at your listeners and avoid faltering and confusion at this crucial moment.

NOTES

1. The flow of topics goes from general to specific. The other direction is OK too, but general-to-specific allows the speech to end with a focus on the audience members' favorite subject—themselves.

2. "The Speechwriter as Candidate." Remarks by Alan M. Perlman to the Chicago Speechwriters Forum, Northfield, IL, April 2, 1996.

3. "The Internet Is the Answer—But What Is the Question?" Keynote remarks by Kathy Olvany Riordan, Director, Media Services, Kraft Foods, Inc., at the Ad Club of New York's "Best Interactive Agencies of 1996" Program, Dec. 18, 1996.

4. Note (1) the conversational language ("Well, that kind of got me to thinking.") and (2) the repetition of *certainty* as an emphatic device.

5. "Building the Bridge to Excellence." Keynote remarks by Robert A. Eckert at the Annual Convention of the National Turkey Federation, San Francisco, CA, Jan. 13, 1997. "Building the Bridge to Excellence" was the theme of the conference.

6. Kraft Foods Supplier Diversity Month Kickoff remarks by Robert S. Morrison, CEO, Kraft Foods, Northfield, IL, Oct. 3, 1996.

4 Economy: Tips for Controlling Length

TIMING YOUR SPEECH

As you come to the end of the composition process, you'll need to start thinking about length and timing. If you're using a script, this is a fairly straightforward matter. Just read a page of text aloud for one minute. Count the number of words you've read (use the Word Count function in your word processor) and multiply that by the number of pages in your script. Alternatively, you can see how long it takes you to read a page (I've found that most people read a double-spaced page of 10-character-per-inch text in 75 to 90 seconds), then multiply by the number of pages.

If you're speaking from notes or bullet points, timing is a little trickier. When your talk is still in the early stages, start rehearsing it, from beginning to end, with a stopwatch.

Do all of this with your time limit in mind. If your speech is too long, you can get it down to the right length—and achieve economy, which is desirable in any event—by applying the techniques in this chapter.

PATHS TO ECONOMY

An economical speech uses as few words as possible. It does-n't tax the audience's endurance or attention span. It's the shortest text that fulfills both the speaker's purposes <u>and</u> the audience's needs.

If you follow my "purpose and audience control content" principle, you're already well on the way toward achieving these goals. Your message, as it begins to take shape, contains only what's necessary, because you have (1) asked yourself, over and over, the purpose and audience questions in the preceding chapter and (2) kept the purpose/audience/content principle in mind and cleared away anything that doesn't conform to it. However, there are two more strategies that will bring you the rest of the way to true economy.

Economy Strategy #1: Eliminate unnecessary words via the NOTHING WHATSOEVER principle.

This technique is appropriate for the times when you need your script to be as compact as possible. Just ask yourself, for every sentence, whether there are words or phrases that contribute NOTHING WHATSOEVER to the meaning.

Watch for phrases with "meaningless" *make, take, is (are),* and *bring.* Phrases such as *give consideration, make an attempt,* and *bring to a conclusion* can be replaced by single words—*consider, try, conclude*—with no loss of meaning. These few examples give you the key to a very large number of cases because the same few empty first words combine with a host of others (*make an estimate* versus *estimate,* and so on). You may be able to snip dozens of unnecessary words—amounting to an entire minute or more—out of your speech.

You can also simplify pairs of words in which one repeats all or part of the meaning of the other, as with *revert back* (*revert* means "turn back"), *basic fundamentals* (fundamentals ARE basic), *seems apparent* (seeming IS appearing), and— my personal favorite—*add additional* (*add* means "provide additional").

An exception to this principle is the use of repetition for emphasis. Repetition is not always unnecessary. It can be a powerful signal of emphasis. For instance:

Neutral list: "We need higher quality, lower cost, and a better return on investment."
Repetition for emphasis: "We need higher quality. We need lower costs. And we need a better return on investment."

Economy Strategy #2: Eliminating unnecessary ideas—text and context.

This second major strategy for achieving economy involves getting rid of everything that your readers can glean from your *text* (because you've already said it or assumed it to be true) or from the *context*—that is, from their education, beliefs, experience, and knowledge of the world.

Eliminating Ideas Available from Your TEXT

For each idea in your speech, ask yourself, "Will my audience remember that I've said this?" If you've already said it, consider deleting it. I say "consider" because if your speech is long and your subject complex or unfamiliar, you may need to intersperse reminders to the audience. The opposite is more often true, however: inexperienced speechmakers repeat themselves far more than they need to.

Part of the reason is that they don't realize how many assumptions can be packed into the meaning of a single word. You don't need to say, "We are pleased with the *progress we have made thus far* in reducing costs." The idea "thus far" is already contained in the word *progress*. Also, *have made* is an empty phrase (if there's progress, somebody has made it). I would drop *have made*; then, to make the grammar come out

right, I'd replace *we* with *our.* The revised version: "We are
pleased with our progress in reducing costs."

Eliminating Ideas Available from CONTEXT
For each idea, ask yourself, "On the basis of their knowledge of the world and of my subject, do my listeners already
know this?" If so—and if they don't need to be reminded—
cut it out.

REVIEW:
PURPOSE/AUDIENCE/CONTENT QUESTIONS

Go back and look over the purpose/content and audience/
content questions in Chapter 1. They should help you identify redundant ideas. It's especially important, as you examine
individual sentences and ideas, to ask,

- ■ **"Will the audience be able to reach this conclusion
  without my help?"** The point here is not to overburden
  your listeners with unnecessary explanations or displays
  of your evidence and reasoning processes.
- ■ **"Is the audience already inclined to believe this?"** You
  don't want to argue eloquently in favor of an obvious
  point that doesn't need much defending.
- ■ **"Does the audience really need to know this?"** Here
  you're asking whether some statement, idea, or point is
  relevant to your purpose (remember, "purpose controls
  content").

WHEN YOU HAVE TO
CUT IT DOWN EVEN MORE

Sometimes—even when you've done all of the above—your
speech is still too long. Don't panic. The good news is that it
really is possible to shorten a text radically. But you have to
make some hard decisions about what's really important.

First, get rid of <u>all</u> repetition.

Then cut out the supporting information (the least important goes first)—illustrative examples, digressions, what-if's, comparisons, and analogies.

If that still doesn't do it, delete the material that seems to serve only your secondary purposes. Relentlessly ask yourself whether the audience needs to know this or that.

Finally, apply the "context" criterion more rigorously—that is, assume a higher level of background knowledge on the part of the audience; that should enable you to get rid of some explanatory material.

It's better if you can deal with these matters while you're still selecting and arranging material. So unless the decision is in your hands, you should *always find out, well in advance, just how long your speech is supposed to be.*

But if you need them, these techniques will work, because the length of a speech is highly elastic. An extreme example: To meet the requirements for a tribute at an anniversary dinner, I once summarized a local philanthropist's lifetime of accomplishments in 25 words.

The key is to realize that not all of your material is equally important. When you have a sense of where each idea stands—whether "most important," "least important," or "somewhere in between"—it becomes much easier to control length.

Quick Credibility: Learning What You Need to Know

Everything I've told you so far will work fine for the cases in which you can pull your subject matter out of your head and your experience. But what happens when part—or even, Heaven forbid, all—of a speechwriting assignment requires you to venture out of your intellectual comfort zone?

No problem. I safely spend most of my time outside my intellectual comfort zone, via the techniques I'm going to show you, techniques that will help you to acquire a quick working knowledge of your subject and to come up with a few pithy generalities on almost any topic.

Read want ads for writers—speech, PR, technical, or what have you—and you'll typically see requirements such as "familiarity with insurance industry a must" or "should have intimate knowledge of soybean industry."

The people who write these ads don't understand what they're advertising for. They think that it's what you know that will make you a good communicator. They're equating education with subject matter, whereas what really counts— especially now, when today's knowledge is obsolete tomorrow—is an agile mind that can locate, absorb, integrate, and evaluate new information.

ELEMENTS OF QUICK CREDIBILITY

Few men make themselves masters of the things they write or speak.

John Selden

You don't have to be a master of the things you're speaking about. But you do have to be credible. And credibility requires that you understand your subject from two perspectives:

1. **Definitional: What it is.**
   You need to understand its historical background, as well as its basic terms, concepts, and current issues, especially the ones of interest to the audience, and their relationships to each other.

2. **Critical: What's important.**
   You need to be able to look at the subject from the audience's point of view and separate the controversial ideas from the widely accepted ones, the ground breaking from the merely interesting, and the interesting from the "ho-hum-what-else-is-new?"

The goal of your research—whether from textbooks, magazines, journals, the Internet/World Wide Web, or all four—is not just to acquire information but to gain these two perspectives on it.

DEFINITIONAL PERSPECTIVE: WHAT IT IS

As you do your reading and Web-browsing, file[1] each piece, as you collect it, according to what it tells you about your main subject.

Description: Pieces that describe, define, or explain your subject or enumerate its parts, components, basic concepts, or characteristics.

Relations: Pieces that show how your subject is partially similar to or different from some other idea (or person, process, etc.), or how it includes another, or how it's actually a part of another.

Variation: Pieces that show how your subject is really equivalent to another—or is an example of it.

Sequence: Pieces that describe the development of your subject or that put it into historical or chronological sequence with others. This file also includes pieces that explain how your subject serves as background for another—or vice versa.

Cause/Effect: Pieces that show how your subject has evolved from or been caused by another—or vice versa.

Consequences: Pieces that show the projected causal outcome, likely effect(s), outlook for, or implications of your subject.

Judgment: Pieces that evaluate your subject—or individual pieces of it, or consequences of it—either in isolation or in comparison to other subjects.

When you organize your incoming material in this way, you're accomplishing three goals: (1) you're organizing your material as you encounter it, thus making it more mentally accessible and helping yourself to learn it; (2) you're becoming aware of the key ideas in your body of subject matter; and (3) you're putting it into categories, at least some of which will correspond to sections of your speech.

Fine, you may be thinking, but when I get all of this done, won't I have enough for a three-hour talk?

You might, but you won't.

As you gather material, you keep in mind your goals and your audience's needs, and you throw out anything that doesn't fit. Also, keep watching for dead ends—ideas that

(1) you don't encounter more than once (which may mean they're off-the-wall, irrelevant, or brilliant—you'll have to figure out which) or that (2) seem to bear no relationship to any of the others (and thus might not really be related to your topic at all).

So you're doing even more than gathering, sorting, arranging, and learning. You're also judiciously selecting what belongs and makes sense—and eliminating what doesn't. As you do, you begin to acquire the second of the two necessary perspectives: the "critical."

CRITICAL PERSPECTIVE: WHAT'S IMPORTANT

As you gather information about your subject, try to get a sense of its key concepts and Big Ideas. (You can do the same with Big Ideas in general if you read widely to stay well informed.[2]) You can acquire this "critical perspective" by observing how each idea is regarded by your various sources. How do they talk about it? How do they position it against other ideas? How new do they think it is? How useful? How well do they think it explains other, seemingly unrelated phenomena?

As you encounter each key concept, answer the above questions and rate the concept according to whatever personal evaluation system works for you. Here's the one I use:[3]

■ **Pre-Buzzwords:** Very new, unproven, and largely unevaluated concepts.

■ **Buzzwords, Stage 1:** Concepts that are positively regarded and widely discussed because of their relevance to—or ability to encapsulate or explain—contemporary events but so new that no specific meaning has been agreed upon. For a while in the 1980s, *competitiveness* was such a buzzword. These are the ideas that well-informed people are just beginning to talk about.

■ **Buzzwords, Stage 2:** Positively regarded, widely discussed words whose meanings are generally agreed upon (but dependent on context); "feel-good" words whose usage is now almost mandatory in any discussion of the larger subject to which they belong (e.g., *reengineering* and *renewal*, which were in the early 1990s—and to some degree still are in the late 1990s—fundamental to discussions of business strategy).

■ **Buzzwords, Stage 3:** Concepts that are still widely used but fading from acceptance and prominence, because they have been either overused or overrated, or both. The examples in Note 3 are Stage 3 buzzwords.

■ **Groundbreakers, Type 1:** Untried concepts that appear to have great promise and problem-solving or explanatory power, perhaps because of their technological sizzle (e.g., the virtual corporation).

■ **Groundbreakers, Type 2:** Concepts that turn out, on the basis of early empirical evidence, to have significance or to be worthy of widespread debate (e.g., the idea of "the end of history," which was supposed to follow the resolution of the Cold War, or the concept "paradigm shift," which seemed to fit so many of the radical changes taking place in the world).

So there you have the key components of quick credibility. Remember: You need more than just a lot of information about your subject.

■ You need various kinds of information about your subject (its parts, consequences, relation to other subjects, and so on).

■ You need to know the terms and concepts that are key to any discussion of it.

■ You need to know the perceived novelty, impact, and usefulness of each key concept.

Do all of this, and you will appear, for all practical purposes, to be an instant expert. Of course, you won't really be an expert, but quick credibility is almost as good. You'll have a working knowledge of your subject—enough, at least, to keep you out of trouble (if you're careful to stay within the limits of your knowledge) and to give the distinct impression that you know what you're talking about.

CREATIVITY ON CUE: GENERATING IDEAS

There's one more of my personal knowledge-acquisition tricks that I'm going to share with you. What do you do when you need some general, valid ideas about a subject—some principles or statements, perhaps even some pithy observations that you can use as an introduction to the specific topic of your speech, or as a summary of your discussion, or even as an aid to organizing your speech?

I've already started to give away the answer. As Winston Churchill once observed, "It is good for an uneducated man to read books of quotations." To that, I would add "and educated men, too—as well as women, whether educated or not."

Collections of quotations aren't just for clergypeople writing sermons. They represent the wisdom of the ages—on a vast variety of subjects, and generally in a hundred words or less.

So if you want some interesting things to say about a subject, begin by collecting a whole bunch of quotes on it.[4] Then arrange them in terms of general themes, by applying "one-level-up" thinking. That is, for each quote, ask yourself, "What idea is this quote an example of?" or "What is the conclusion that can be drawn from this quote?"

Let's say you're writing a speech about change and you want to include some generalities that you'll connect to your audience or the topic at hand.

You start to review the quotes you've collected, and you encounter a Japanese proverb: "If you sit on a stone for three years you will get used to it." One level up: "We have to acknowledge the need for change."

Then you see this comment by Elbert Hubbard, the 19th-century writer and editor: "The world is moving so fast these days that the man who says it can't be done is generally interrupted by someone doing it." Aha! Change is rapid.

Here's one from the famous sage "Anonymous": "Dealing with change is like giving up smoking and drinking and going on a diet, all at the same time." Change is difficult.

Then you see the words of management consultant Tom Peters: "Today, loving change, tumult, even chaos, is a prerequisite for survival, let alone success." Change is necessary.

Author James Baldwin's observation that "the future is like heaven—everyone exalts it, but no one wants to go there now" tells us much the same thing as Anonymous did.

How about "The future never just happened. It was created" (Will and Ariel Durant)? That's a new theme: change is driven by conscious choices.

This from Confucius: "Whosoever adapteth himself shall be preserved to the end." Same as Tom Peters. So Tom's getting the big bucks for recycling ancient wisdom!

Now you're getting the idea. You'll see the same themes repeated in different ways, as sages in each era discover the same basic truths. And after you've reviewed 50 or 60 quotes on a subject, you'll find as many as a dozen or more good ideas, verified by wisdom and experience, that you can use in your speech.

To see how I worked these ideas into a speech text, go back to Chapter 1 and look at the second example under Audience/Content Question #2.

Here's another. All the main points came from the quotes about art that I found in various books.

The whole process of artistic creation is strange and marvelous, especially to us business types, who always start out with so many "givens."

The actual execution of a work of art is just as mysterious. How in the world was the artist able to paint or sculpt his or her vision in just that way, with such perfect form and balance, such a perfect blend of color, line, and shape? But although these mysteries do intrigue me, I don't spend a lot of time worrying about them . . . mainly because I'm too busy appreciating what you artists actually have accomplished.

To begin with, **your works of art often impose some sort of pattern on our experience; they somehow put things into orderly relationships.** In a world where the sheer variety and complexity of our lives is sometimes almost overwhelming, that's a pretty remarkable accomplishment.

I also find that **you artists often show me something I couldn't have imagined—something I never knew was there; your limitless imagination makes up for the limits of my own.** In a world where we're so preoccupied with immediate, everyday reality, that's another remarkable accomplishment.

Something else that artists do . . . is to capture a feeling, an emotion, or some other elusive element of life. In a world where we hurry from one thing to the next so rapidly that we often miss a lot of the experiences that make it all worthwhile . . . that too is a remarkable accomplishment.

Finally, **you artists reveal yourselves to us. Through your works, you tell us who you are, and you show us your highly original reactions to the world.** Then we can look at what you've done and say, "Yes! That's exactly what I feel!" . . . or, "No, that's not my feeling at all." But no matter how we respond, you've made us think—and you've built a bridge between one human being and another. And in a world where we spend so much energy <u>hiding</u> our private selves . . . that is one more remarkable accomplishment.

POSTSCRIPT:
THE EFFECTIVE USE OF QUOTES

Of course, you might want to use quotes in the more conventional manner, to introduce a point you're making, or to summarize it, or to support or confirm it (as if to imply, "Look! Even Confucius agrees with me."). A few pieces of advice:

■ **Less is more.** Two or three well-chosen quotes are better than six or eight that distract from your message and make your audience wonder whether you have any original thoughts.

■ **Make sure the quote is functional**—that it really does support, introduce, and so on, and in a vivid way. If the quote does not add value to your speech with its pithy conciseness or sparkling originality but merely repeats what you've said, skip it.

■ **You don't have to use the whole thing.** If the quote is long, pick only the part that's truly relevant to your speech and that performs the function you want it to perform (but please, don't do any editing or rewriting; if the language is archaic, obscure, or sexist, find another quote—or amend it in your own words, as I did with the Churchill quote above).

■ **Take great care in setting up the quote and identifying the person who said it.** Make an educated guess as to your audience's knowledge base, and proceed accordingly. Nobody needs to be told who Confucius was, although you can give a little historical perspective: "Over two thousand years ago, Confucius wrote . . . " An audience of business people will know who Tom Peters is, but an audience of, say, church laypeople may have to hear something like, "According to management consultant Tom Peters . . . " If you've got a great quote by someone really obscure, you can lead with "A very wise person once observed that . . . "

And—very important—since your listeners don't know that a quote is coming, you must prepare them with extra words, as I just did with Confucius and Tom Peters. Don't just say, "Tom Peters said . . . "—it goes by too fast, and it's too easy to miss.

■ Consider adding a little "coda" (or exit comment) to the quote—a signal that it's over and that now you're speaking again, for example, "He was so right," or, "That's so true," or, "That pretty much says it all, doesn't it?" Or you might relate the quote to your audience or to the topic at hand. For example, after the Japanese proverb, you might say, "And what stones are we sitting on? What have we gotten used to?"

NOTES

1 A "file" can be either physical (e.g., manila folder) or electronic.

2. If you can acquire a critical perspective on general knowledge, you'll be equipped to write speeches on a wide range of subjects (as indeed we professional ghostwriters do). This is, of course, a more formidable task than writing on one subject. But it's largely a matter of time and experience: the better informed you are overall, the easier it becomes to assess the perceived value and impact of each new idea and thus to tell the extent to which it seems a real Big Idea (see Appendix for a recommended reading list). And if your speeches contain references to current events or ideas (notice how many of my examples do just that), they'll sound more fresh and interesting, and they'll be connected to the world that you and your listeners share.

3. It's very hard to give examples here, because each category involves a time component. What was a Type 1 Buzzword when this chapter was first written may have moved to Type 3 by the time it's read.

These examples of mid-'90s buzzwords (from *Forbes*, 2/20/95) reveal buzzwords in their final stages of development; the facetious "definitions" show that the words and phrases have been around long enough that their original meanings have been (deliberately and cynically) misinterpreted.

Team player: An employee who substitutes the thinking of the herd for his own good judgment.

Reengineering: The principal slogan of the Nineties, used to describe any and all corporate strategies.

Vision: Top management's heroic guess about the future, easily printed on mugs, T-shirts, posters, and calendar cards.

Paradigm shift: A euphemism companies use when they realize the rest of their industry has expanded into Guangdong while they were investing in Orange County.

Restructuring: A simple plan instituted from above, in which workers are rightsized, downsized, surplused, lateralized or, in the business jargon of yore, fired.

Empowerment: A magic wand management waves to help traumatized survivors of restructuring suddenly feel engaged, self-managed, and in control of their futures and their jobs.

4. Half a dozen recent quote books should be all you need to start with (see Appendix). I always buy them for myself, because I don't have time to go to the library, and most libraries don't have many good recent ones. One-stop-shopping for quotations—as well as anecdotes, humor, and much else—is possible on-line, with IdeaBank, the source of all the quotations in this section [11 Joan Drive, Chappaqua, NY 10514; (914) 666-4211, home page http://www.idea-bank.com].

APPENDIX
AIDS TO QUICK CREDIBILITY:
SOURCES OF FACTS, QUOTES, AND
OTHER USEFUL MATERIAL

Asimov, Isaac. *Isaac Asimov's Book of Facts.* New York: Bell Publishing, 1979.

Asimov, Isaac, and Shulman, Jason A. *Isaac Asimov's Book of Science and Nature Quotations.* New York: Weidenfeld & Nicolson, 1979.

Brewer, Ebenezer Cobham. *Brewer's Dictionary of Phrase and Fable.* New York: Harper & Row, 1970. Contains origins of many common phrases.

Brussel, Eugene E. *Dictionary of Quotable Definitions.* New York: Prentice-Hall, 1970. Contains mostly quotes that are in the form of definitions.

Butler, Paul F., and George, John. *They Never Said It: A Book of Fake Quotes, Misquotes and Misleading Attributions.* New York: Oxford University Press, 1990.

Cerf, Christopher, and Navasky, Victor. *The Experts Speak: The Definitive Compendium of Authoritative Misinformation.* New York: Pantheon Books, 1984. An extraordinarily useful collection of statements and predictions on a wide variety of subjects—all of which turned out to be wrong.

Chase's Annual Events. Chicago: Contemporary Publishing Company. Published annually; contains information about each date and month of the year, as well as birthdays of famous people.

Cohen, J.M., and Cohen, M.J. *The Penguin Dictionary of Modern Quotations.* New York: Penguin Books, 1981.

Dachman, Ken. *Newswordy: A Contemporary Encyclopedia of People, Places, Events & Words in the Headlines.* New York: Simon and Schuster, 1985.

Eigen, Lewis D., and Siegel, Jonathan P. *The Manager's Book of Quotations.* New York: Amacom (division of American Management Association), 1989.

Fadiman, Clifton. *The Little, Brown Book of Anecdotes.* Boston: Little, Brown, 1985.

Feldman, David. *Imponderables: The Solution to the Mysteries of Everyday Life*. New York: Morrow, 1986.

Fitzhenry, Robert I. *Barnes & Noble Book of Quotations*. New York: Harper and Row, 1983.

Fulghum, Robert. *Everything I Really Need to Know I Learned in Kindergarten: Uncommon Thoughts on Common Things*. New York: G.K. Hall, 1988.

Griffith, Joe. *Speaker's Library of Business Stories, Anecdotes and Humor*. New York: Prentice Hall, 1990.

Gross, John. *The Oxford Book of Aphorisms*. Oxford: Oxford University Press, 1987. Another good book of quotations—but learned and literary.

Grun, Bernard. *The Timetables of History: A Horizontal Linkage of People and Events*. New York: Simon & Schuster, 1982.

Hay, Peter. *The Book of Business Anecdotes*. New York: Facts on File Publications, 1988.

Hirsch, E.D., Kett, Joseph F., and Trefil, James. *The Dictionary of Cultural Literacy™: What Every American Should Know*. Boston: Houghton Mifflin, 1988.

Iapoce, Michael. *A Funny Thing Happened on the Way to the Boardroom: Using Humor in Business Speaking*. New York: John Wiley & Sons, 1988.

Kent, Robert W. *Money Talks: The 2500 Greatest Business Quotations from Aristotle to DeLorean*. New York: Facts on File Publications, 1985.

Maggio, Rosalie. *The Beacon Book of Quotations by Women*. Boston: Beacon Press, 1992.

Metcalf, Fred. *The Penguin Dictionary of Modern Humorous Quotation*. London: Penguin Books, 1987.

Moyers, Bill D. *A World of Ideas: Conversations with Thoughtful Men and Women*. New York: Doubleday, 1989.

Panati, Charles. *Extraordinary Origins of Everyday Things*. New York: Harper and Row, 1987.

Peter, Laurence J. *Peter's Quotations: Ideas for Our Times*. Toronto: Bantam Books, 1980.

Platt, Suzy. *Respectfully Quoted: A Dictionary of Quotations Requested from the Congressional Research.* Washington, D.C.: Library of Congress, 1989.

Rheingold, Howard, and Levine, Howard. *Talking Tech: A Conversational Guide to Science and Technology.* New York: Quill, 1983.

Robertson, Patrick. *The Book of Firsts.* New York: Bramhall House, 1982.

Safir, Leonard, and Safire, William. *Good Advice.* New York: NY Times Books, 1982.

Safire, William, and Safir, Leonard. *Leadership.* New York: Simon and Schuster, 1990.

Telushkin, Joseph. *Uncommon Sense: The World's Fullest Compendium of Wisdom.* New York: Shapolsky, 1986.

Tomlinson, Gerald. *Speaker's Treasury of Sports Anecdotes, Stories and Humor.* New York: Prentice Hall, 1990.

Tripp, Rhonda Thomas. *The International Thesaurus of Quotations.* New York: Thomas Y. Crowell, 1970.

Wentworth, Harold, and Flexner, Stuart Berg. *Dictionary of American Slang.* New York: Thomas Y. Crowell, 1975.

Winokur, Jon. *The Portable Curmudgeon.* New York: New American Library, 1987.

6 Ceremonial Speeches

WHY CEREMONIAL SPEECHES ARE DIFFERENT

Ceremonial speeches are words that accompany real-world events. Sometimes they actually make those events happen. When a judge "pronounces" two people husband and wife, they are husband and wife. And when that same judge "sentences" someone to five to ten in the slammer, all the resources of the State are then put to work to get that person to the appropriate penal institution—and keep him or her there.

Sometimes you may be called upon to utter the right words so that something can happen. You <u>introduce</u> another person to an audience, you <u>dedicate</u> something, you <u>accept</u> an award—in every case, the word describes what you're doing when you utter it.

The trouble is, you can't just say the one sentence and be done with it. You've got to say something else. But what? This chapter will help you answer that question.

THE CHALLENGE

Ceremonial speeches <u>are</u> tough to write—no doubt about it. If we can understand why this is, we'll have taken the first step toward making them easier—and maybe even a little more fun.

In the first place, the goals of the ceremonial speech are uncertain. True, we do get some guidance from the words that characterize the different types of speech: *introduce, dedi-cate, accept*. And indeed the audience gets a very satisfying sense of closure—a sense that the purpose of the speech has been accomplished—if, somewhere near the end, you actually use the relevant word: "It's a pleasure to introduce . . . ," "I dedicate . . . ," "I accept . . .". But we still come back to the original question: Aside from its ostensible purpose, what is the speech supposed to accomplish?

Another problem is content. What should the ceremonial speech say? This is related to the previous problem, since pur-pose controls content. What you seek to accomplish by com-municating determines what you will actually say or write.

Finally, there's the problem of arousing and holding the audience's interest. How do you link the ceremonial speech to your listeners' concerns? Why should they care about what is taking place? What is its significance to them?

The good news is that in writing ceremonial speeches, we have many different ways to be creative. So let's look at the major types of ceremonial speeches—and see just what and where these opportunities are.

INTRODUCTIONS[1]

General Strategies: The Goals of the Introductory Speech

Your introductory speech should accomplish three goals:

1. It should give the audience a sense of the speaker's topic.
2. It should familiarize the audience with the speaker's per-sonality and accomplishments, especially those that are relevant to his or her topic. It should do this in an inter-esting way, by weaving together the dry biographical essentials (which need not be in strict chronological order), the pertinent personal and anecdotal material, and

the items that are relevant to the audience (current events, accomplishments of the speaker's organization, and others).

3. It should create a sense of anticipation for both speaker and topic. When the speaker gets up to talk, the listeners should be on the edge of their seats.

Introductions: Doing the Research

First, gather a respectable amount of information on the speaker and his or her personality and accomplishments. Consult data bases, research services, or the speaker's office, press agent, or PR firm. Talk to people who know the speaker. I don't mean extensive interviewing. You need only five to seven minutes worth of material—not a biography. But very often, you'll ask that press-office or PR person (or whoever sends you the written material), "What kind of a person is he/she?" and you'll get a couple of personal qualities or anecdotes—little nuggets you can really use.

If the speaker is a CEO, consult *Business Week*'s "Corporate Elite," the magazine's annual issue on CEOs. There you'll find short profiles that can give you leads for further research. Also, send for the company's annual report and check out your speaker's Letter to Shareholders. That will tell you something about your speaker's priorities and accomplishments.

One way or another, you've got to get hold of feature articles or profiles of your speaker. These will enable you to transcend the standard biographical material and give your listeners a well-rounded picture of the person they're about to hear. How do you know when you have enough material? Simple: When you see non-biographical items (such as the speaker's personal qualities or particular anecdotes about him/her) repeated from one source to the next, it's time to stop collecting.

As you go through your materials, read actively. Look for specific personality characteristics; intellectual, political, or managerial strengths; and endorsements from others whose words describe the speaker's positive qualities. As you find them, key them to your sources by letter (each letter denotes one of your source documents) and number (for each excerpt). Also, put each letter/number pair on a master sheet, by topic. For example, if you write, "Quick wit, ready sense of humor—A/6, B/2, D/7," on your master sheet, that means that you found three references to your speaker's sense of humor: the sixth excerpt in your first source, the second in source #2, and so on.

As you do your research, stay loose. Don't go into it with any preconceived notion of what kind of picture will emerge. Instead, things will go much faster and smoother if you let the research shape the speech. Thus, if you run across a piece—an interview, let's say—that contains the speaker's philosophy of life, business, or whatever he/she will be talking about, then you have an excellent possibility for the focus of the introduction, as in this example:

> I think the key to understanding John is to realize that he operates according to a very specific and fully formed philosophy of business success—one that he's polished and refined through years of observation and practice. He lives by a small set of ideas that, taken together, are a forceful, pragmatic crystallization of volumes of practical management wisdom.
>
> Let me give you a few samples, all of them quotes from published interviews with John himself.
>
>> Start small and set short-term goals. Great dreams are often so far from your reach that you can become discouraged, but each small goal you achieve gives you confidence to try for the next.

You have to be willing to change your mind when new information comes along. Keep your options open.

The general ought to lead the army. In business, top managers should lead by example. I never ask people to solve problems I couldn't solve, and I work only on projects that others have failed at.

Success requires "active patience"; while you're being patient, you're also trying every conceivable way of making things happen. (By the way, that reminds me of Thomas Edison's remark that "everything comes to him who hustles while he waits.")

Failure is a word I don't accept.

If there is any secret to our success, it is that we have changed with the times. Perhaps we should think in terms of "responsible daring": we have to anticipate what the reader wants by walking a step ahead of him.

And finally, let me give you two of my favorites . . . two maxims that I think complete this little sketch of John Johnson and provide the most telling insights into him and his achievements.

First, John says, "Once I decide I'm really going to do something, I psych myself up and convince myself that I'm going to do it. And in effect I gain confidence expressing confidence. But I think it's very important to live with fear. One of the things that fear tells you is that you care about what you're doing."

And second: "People go on vacation to do exactly what they would like to do. By that definition, I'm on vacation all the time."

Notice how the "philosophy of business/life" introduction is set up so that it flatters the speaker and tells the listeners that the speaker is going to help them understand the person they're about to hear:

I think the key to understanding John is to realize that he operates according to a very specific and fully formed philosophy of business success—one that he's polished and refined through years of observation and practice.

But don't go into it thinking, "This person's philosophy of life must be interesting—I'm going to dig it up." You can't let the success of the project hinge on something that may not be available.

Introductions: General Principles

1. Finesse the Obvious

If important biographical details are already familiar to most of the audience, preface them with "As we all know . . ." or some similar expression—then give them:

I have a most enjoyable job to do this afternoon. And as I was preparing for it, I was reminded of another introduction. This one was so mediocre that when it was over, the speaker got up and said, "Well . . . of all the introductions I've ever received . . . that was the most recent."

I certainly hope that won't happen today. When you're bringing on a man of John Johnson's stature, you just can't get up and read his resume. You do that, and you're going to put everyone in the audience right on the edge of a deep slumber.

After all, **we all know** that John is the head of a multibillion-dollar publishing and cosmetics empire.

And **most of us are probably aware** that he's Chairman and CEO of the Supreme Life Insurance Company . . . that he's a trustee of the Art Institute of Chicago and the United Negro College Fund, among others . . . that he's received 20 honorary doctorates, been inducted into the Chicago Business Hall of

Fame, and been named the Most Outstanding Black
Publisher in History.

2. Watch Length Carefully

The task is to introduce the speaker, not give a speech of
your own. Your introduction should be long enough to build
the audience's enthusiasm—but no longer. That's three to five
minutes, seven at the most.

I mention this because you do have to get into your
speaker's life and accomplishments enough so that you yourself are excited and can convey that excitement to the audience. But it may turn out that your speaker is a superachiever
whom you really admire and—as has happened to me more
than once—you get so caught up in the person's accomplishments that you just have to tell them all.

So be selective. You achieve optimal length by pruning
away everything that's irrelevant to the audience, the occasion, and the speaker's topic—unless you have compelling
reasons to do otherwise.

3. Be Relentlessly Positive

Never miss a chance to pay a personal compliment to the
speaker, as long as you can do so sincerely, based on either
your interviews or your written sources.

Conversely—and it almost goes without saying—make sure
your introduction contains nothing that is derogatory, conde-
scending, or uncomplimentary in any way. Questions about
the speaker's health, competence, or ethics—even if ground-
less, even if amusing—are better left unspoken. The same goes
for career setbacks like flunking out of college. Humorous anecdotes are fine—as long as they reflect positively on the speaker.

4. Try to Build Suspense

Have fun with the opening. Build suspense. Find something interesting about your speaker (in the example below, it's

the fact that he was the president's first choice for his team), then generalize that to everyday life—and begin with it. Make the audience wonder where you're going—then close in briskly on your speaker and his/her topic, as in this example:

> There's an interesting ritual associated with informal team sports. You see it in gym classes, in public parks, and everywhere that boys and girls get together for a game of basketball, baseball, or whatever. It's called "choosing up sides," and we've all had to submit to it at one time or another. There you stand, knowing that the order in which you're chosen is a direct reflection of how good the captain thinks you are. Our speaker today was the very first member that the president chose for his team—and that gives you a pretty clear idea of the captain's opinion of him.

Introductions: Writing the Opening

Here are some devices and strategies for writing the beginning of your introduction.

Use a Quote

Look for a gem of a quote about your speaker—and use it as a springboard for much or all of your introduction, as in

> One year and eleven days ago, our guest speaker became chairman of General Foods—the company's youngest CEO in 30 years. The *Chicago Tribune* called him "one of the most versatile and multitalented executives to reach the company's top office."
> It's not difficult to see why the paper came to that conclusion.

Go from General to Specific

Begin with the speaker's organization, cause, or topic. Tell the audience what it is and why it's important. Then move from that into a discussion of the speaker:

The man we'll be hearing from tonight . . . recently
became head of The Nature Conservancy, a private, nonprofit international organization whose environmental
strategy does work. That strategy is based on a simple,
rational premise: to really control what happens to the
land, you must control the land itself. So The Nature
Conservancy doesn't spend a lot of money litigating or
lobbying; it spends a lot of money buying land.

Its mission is to protect the best examples of ecosys-
tems and endangered species. Since its founding in
1951, the Conservancy has been responsible for the pro-
tection of over 5 million acres in the 50 states, Canada,
Latin America, and the Caribbean. With all its land, The
Conservancy now owns and manages the largest pri-
vately owned nature preserve system in the world.

Then move from that into a discussion of the speaker
him/herself:

Our speaker became president and CEO of this remarkable
organization earlier this year. It's the latest move in a
career that has seen him move back and forth between
academia and government, then into private consulting.
And everywhere he has gone, this quiet, intense, enormously capable man has made a big difference.

Another, more subtle way to go from general to specific is
to identify something noteworthy about your speaker, then
lead into it by moving from the general to the specific. In this
approach, you portray the noteworthy item as an example of
something we encounter in daily life—that's the "general"
part—then get specific by explaining the relevance to the
speaker. For example:

We Americans are great joiners and great admirers of
individual achievement . . . which is why we have so
many fan clubs. We have fan clubs for real people like

the Beach Boys and Elvis . . . and for not-so-real people
like James Bond. We have fan clubs for sports teams,
soap operas, and *Star Trek.*

But how many politicians have their own organized following of admirers and alumni? Our speaker
today does: There is actually a group of prominent
young movers and shakers in Indiana, all of whom
have two things in common—at some point in their
careers, they worked for Richard Lugar . . . and they
continue to appreciate the abilities of their former
mentor and chief. They hold an annual "Chickenfest"
that draws as many as 250 people. As one of them
says, "Once you've worked for Lugar, you've got a
sense of the intellectual cream of the crop."

To me, all of this says a lot about Dick Lugar himself.

Birthdays and Birth-Mates

Check *Chase's Annual Events* (see the Appendix, previous
chapter) to see who has the same birthday as your speaker.
You might find that the speaker has something else in common with his/her "birth-mates":

Now, I usually don't introduce a person by starting with
his birth date, but in this case, there's an interesting
coincidence: Frank Jones was born on February 6—the
same day as Ronald Reagan. And he shares with President Reagan a belief in the power of free markets and
the effectiveness of private-sector solutions.

Or you can speculate as to what they might have in
common:

Now, I don't want to take this birthday thing too far—
but I should point out that February 6 is also the birthday of some other illustrious figures in our nation's history: Aaron Burr, Babe Ruth, and Zsa Zsa Gabor. Our
guest today may be as controversial as Burr . . . as heroic

as Ruth . . . and as glamorous as Gabor. So why don't I just bring him on, so that you can see for yourselves?

Conference Theme

If your speaker is part of a program or conference, begin with some remarks on the theme of the conference, then tie the speaker's remarks to it.

Ultimate Impact

Look at the connection between the speaker's organization, cause, or key concern . . . and its ultimate impact. If it's unusual, obscure, or indirect, then put organization/cause/concern and ultimate impact together in the form of a riddle. Admit the obscurity—then explain the real relevance:

> Let me begin my introduction of our guest speaker by posing a question for you: What does the Library of Congress have to do with America's competitiveness in world markets?
>
> Now, if I'd asked you that 10 or 15 years ago, you might have been a little confused. Once upon a time, the connection between a nation's central library and its economic performance might have seemed so obscure that my question might have come across as some sort of off-the-wall riddle.
>
> But not today—not in 1990. Our world is growing more complex and interdependent with each passing year . . . and productivity and innovation are fast becoming the hallmarks of national greatness. In the world I've just described, the intellectual abilities of our people are, more than ever, the key to our country's future.

And if the connection simply amounts to a rediscovery of old wisdom, so much the better. Say so—and support your assertion with an appropriate quote:

And we are rediscovering the truth of what Thomas Jefferson, the founder of the Library of Congress, wrote almost 180 years ago: "If a nation expects to be ignorant and free, in a state of civilization, it expects what never was and never will be."

Our speaker today is a passionate believer that Jefferson's ideas possess a new and urgent relevance to an age of electronic information.

Business Connection

Relate the speaker's business to that of your organization or company.

"And He Was So Right!"

Look for cases in which your speaker's philosophies, positions, or policies turned out to be correct—or even prophetic.

In 1860, for example, the Republican candidate for president, a fellow named Abraham Lincoln, said that the South "has too much common sense and good temper to break up the Union." Sorry, Abe; I wish you had been right about that one. As it turned out, you weren't, and as the recent PBS television series on the Civil War showed us, the result was horrible almost beyond imagination . . .

Now, the reason why I bring all of this up is that once again we face the possibility of war—and mere months after some so-called experts even announced "the end of history": from now on, they felt, competing ideologies would no longer have the power to send people into battle; it would just be a matter of fine-tuning the economic and political systems we have.

Well, I wish the experts had been right. But our speaker tonight was—and is—a realist about such things. And for a while, he was a very lonely voice calling for a strong national defense, despite the general euphoria about the end of the Cold War. He called the Congress a bunch of naive optimists who had "decided to give away their overcoats on the first sunny day in January." I think he knew all along what so many of us have recently been reminded of: it's a difficult and dangerous world out there . . . one in which armed might—though never the most desirable choice—must nevertheless remain one of America's options.

Speaker/Introducer Connection

If you and the speaker have anything positive in common (hobbies, career progress or events, travel, birthplace, business/political philosophy), use that as a reason for the introducer's enthusiasm—and, by extension, as a reason why the audience should feel enthusiasm.

HOW TO ORGANIZE
THE INTRODUCTION

Here are two different ways to organize your introduction.

1. Enumerate the Positives

Try to make each of the speaker's positive characteristics or strengths the topic sentence of a paragraph. Then fill the rest of the paragraph with biographical or anecdotal material that demonstrates the validity of the topic sentence:

> [CHARACTERISTIC:] Ross Perot is a triumphant entrepreneur in the best of the American tradition . . . [ILLUSTRATIONS:] from his humble beginnings in Texas, delivering newspapers on horseback . . . to the presidency of his class at the U.S. Naval Academy . . . to an exceptional sales career at IBM . . . to the founding of his own company, EDS.
> [CHARACTERISTIC:] Ross is also a business leader. [ILLUSTRATIONS:] The company he started mirrors his own entrepreneurial vigor, with its aggressive, can-do culture. His loyalty to his employees—and theirs to

him—is legendary. EDS is an organization that embodies and continues the founder's fiery spirit. It's an organization that every other firm can look to and learn
from.

Ross has planted the seed of his energy in the fertile
soil of American opportunity. [CHARACTERISTIC:]
And he has not hesitated to share the fruits of his success. [ILLUSTRATIONS:] His generosity is measured in
the tens of millions of dollars. It has bought tangible
items like a new park or a symphony hall . . . as well as
support for causes that he believes in. We're all aware
of his daring plan, back in 1979, to rescue two of his
employees held prisoner in Iran . . . and of his humanitarian efforts on behalf of American POWs, MIAs, and,
as we've recently learned, hostages in the Middle East.

[CHARACTERISTIC:] Ross is a fighter on the side
of American business and industry. [ILLUSTRATION:]
Everything he says and does is aimed at making our
nation a more formidable competitor. And in that
cause, I am his staunch ally. Ross and I may not see eye
to eye on how to get things done—but we do agree on
what needs to be done.

[CHARACTERISTIC:] Finally, Ross is a remarkable
human being. [ILLUSTRATION:] When you sort
through all the ventures and exploits—and all the
myths and legends that have grown up around them—
you find, at bottom, a simple, generous man of rock-
solid principles . . . a man with the relatively rare ability to identify a goal that's worth pursuing—and then
pursue it with bulldog tenacity. In that, Ross bears a
distinct resemblance to Winston Churchill, the man
whose name is on the award that Ross received last
February. It honors individuals of exceptional accomplishment—people who demonstrate "the imagination,
boldness and vigor which characterized Churchill."

The more important the characteristic, the more time you
should spend on it.

As you enumerate the positive, be sure to connect your speaker's experience with his/her topic, so as to add to the speaker's credibility (in this next example, the characteristic <u>follows</u> the illustrations):

> [ILLUSTRATIONS:] Our speaker serves on a variety of boards and commissions, including the Business Round-table, the Conference Board, the Bretton Woods Committee, and the International Trade Policy Committee. He served on the presidentially appointed Advisory Committee for Trade Negotiations. [CHARACTERISTIC:] Clearly, his thoughts on trade policy, which he'll be sharing with us today, come from a wealth of first-hand experience.

2. Biography, Then Personality

When you organize your introduction in this way, you first give the highlights of your speaker's life and career; you then talk about him/her as a person. Make a sharp, clear transition between the two. Something like, "Well, so much for what our speaker is. Now what can I tell you about <u>who</u> he is?" And put the personal part last, as if to say, "<u>This</u> is what's really important."

Introductions: Summarize and Build to a Climax

The ending is key. It must build to a climax. Ideally, it should raise the listeners' sense of anticipation to the point where they just can't wait to hear your speaker. It should summarize the speaker's strengths, virtues, and accomplishments. For example:

> What it all comes down to is that Frank Jones represents that all-too-rare combination of thinker, doer, and leader, and this—plus all of his expertise and experience in energy and the environment—makes him practically

a natural resource unto himself! I know you'll join me in wishing him every success in his new job . . . and in welcoming him tonight.

Ladies and gentlemen . . . the president and chief executive officer of The Nature Conservancy . . . Dr. Frank Jones.

Perhaps you can find a quote that reveals, in a concise and pithy way, just how important those strengths and accomplishments are. If you have more than one quote, save the most telling one for the ending. This example uses two quotes, one to lead into and one to cap off the finale. (Remember: build to a climax.)

There's an old proverb that says, "If you wish to know what a man is, place him in authority." Well, as Dave has risen from one level to the next, we've seen exactly what he is. He is a superb business manager. And he is an enthusiastic, confident leader who understands the dynamics of a tightly competitive, global industry— and knows how to be successful in it. As *Business Week* put it, he is "the right man for the right time."

Introductions: The Climax

Stretch out that final-final sentence with the speaker's full name and full title, plus—if appropriate as in the example above—a personal aside:

Please join me in welcoming . . . the president and chief operating officer of General Foods . . . and a man I'm proud to call my colleague and friend . . . Josiah Carberry.

Your final sentence should contain a clear APPLAUSE sign—for example, "Please join me in welcoming," . . . or, "It's a pleasure to welcome." For variations, listen to the way

entertainers introduce people. These are the formulas that
your audience expects to hear.

DEDICATIONS[2]

This category includes dedications of buildings, monuments,
and other facilities, as well as speeches at ground-breakings,
ribbon-cuttings, and unveilings, plus speeches for anniversaries, commemorations, and other milestones (such as the
millionth product to come off an assembly line).

Two general principles:

1. **Tell them why they're there.** Be specific about <u>what</u>
   they're celebrating or commemorating.
2. At the end, **complete the act of dedicating** by dedicating
   <u>to</u> something or somebody (if possible, three somethings
   or somebodies; using three items always sounds better
   and carries more impact):

   > So today, August 21, 1987, we dedicate this marker to
   > Charles Packard . . . to his vision of building "one car-
   > riage in as nearly perfect a manner as possible" . . .
   > and the millions of outstanding Packards—and, more
   > importantly, to the generations of Packard <u>people</u>—
   > that have made that vision a reality.

Aside from these generalities, there's no one formula I can
give you, since there are so many things that are dedicated,
for so many different reasons. But the variety of situations
means that any of a variety of approaches can work for you.

Talk in General Terms about the Occasion Itself

How do you link this <u>specific</u> event with the more <u>general</u>
concepts of welcoming, dedicating, or celebrating anniversaries?

Why do we make such a big deal of anniversaries? Well, last month, the *Wall Street Journal* did an article on the subject. And according to a professor who was quoted in the *Journal,* marking milestones "provides us with a tie to the past while at the same time giving us an opportunity to reexperience. [It allows] us to share our cultural traditions with others and with our younger generations."

I can't think of a better explanation of our festivities today. And so that's what I'd like to do: I'd like to "reexperience" with you some of our company's traditions . . . and talk a little about how these traditions tie the remarkable triumphs of our past to our bright hopes for its future.

Global View

Take a global view. Explain how what you're dedicating fits in with or fulfills some larger plan.

Of all the many issues that we deal with in Corporate Affairs, few are more emotional than food safety. And rightly so: every time a consumer takes a bite of one of our products, he or she commits an act of faith. That faith, that trust, intangible though they may be, are nevertheless one of the foundations of the success of our business, and we must do everything we can to justify and strengthen them.

The greenhouse we're dedicating today will help us to do just that. Kraft General Foods is a strong supporter of the research that's going on here, and The Land already has the best integrated pest management program in the country for greenhouse food production. The research that goes on in this new facility will ultimately teach us even more about how to make food safe. It will help us to deploy a broad arsenal of weapons against the pests that threaten our food supply.[3]

Talk Symbolically

What does the thing you're dedicating stand for? What is its larger meaning?

> That's why I'm delighted to dedicate this facility. It symbolizes the synergy of traditional manufacturing and modern systems engineering . . . the spirit of innovation that runs deep in both of our organizations . . . and the progress that we've made—and will continue to make—together.

New Facility, Same People

If you're dedicating a new facility staffed by current employees, tell them, in one way or another, that this is their day.

To the extent possible, credit them for achievements in the old facility—or for what they've accomplished so far in the new one. Talk about what has (or has not) changed.

This is a very effective approach because it enables you to show familiarity—and thus to bond—with your audience, but it must be executed with care. You'll need to get authentic local flavor from someone on the scene.

AWARD ACCEPTANCES

General Strategy: Modesty above All

You're being honored—in fact, the award citation may be downright lavish in its praise—so appear modest. I suggest two ways to do this:

1. Quote someone on modesty or humility: "At moments like this, I remember a piece of advice from Golda Meir: 'Don't be so humble,' she said. 'You're not that great.'"

2. Find someone else to share the glory with. Who? That's easy: Just ask yourself who actually did the real nuts-and-bolts work that you—through your monetary contributions, your organizational or administrative work, or your supervision—have set in motion or made possible. Or—and this is the familiar Oscar/Emmy/Grammy gambit—share credit with whoever helped make you worthy of the award.

A variation on this theme is to accept on behalf of someone else:

> Thank you very much for this award. I accept, with pleasure and gratitude . . . and I do so not just for myself, but also on behalf of all the true leaders in my company and throughout American business and industry—in recognition of all that they have done to maintain the conscience of our corporations and to promote human dignity and social justice.

Content of the Acceptance Speech: Specific Strategies

Use one or more of these, as the occasion allows.

Talk about the Cause

If the award represents excellence or achievement in—or advancement of—a cause, offer perspective on that.

> Thanks, Jim, for those kind words. I'm very grateful for this recognition. But there are many others whom we also ought to acknowledge tonight. So I accept this award on behalf—and in appreciation—of the many thousands of General Foods people who have responded to the call of their conscience . . . and who, through their monetary support and their everyday behavior at home and on the job, have furthered the

cause of interracial and interfaith brotherhood and sisterhood here in Westchester County.

I'd like to give you my perspective on the progress of that cause. How are we doing? And where do we go from here?

Interpret the Event; Praise the Values

Explain the event at which the award is being presented: what are we really doing here? As you do, you can also interpret the meaning of the award itself: give your listeners some idea of the importance of the values that are being recognized.

What we're doing here today is more than an awards ceremony, as enjoyable as that is . . . and more than a fundraising event, as important as that is to the future of Scouting. By singling out Good Scouts, we send a message that "this is the kind of society we want to have"—a society that respects individual achievement and takes pride in the values associated with Scouting itself.

This is another way for you to appear modest: the real issues transcend you—you're part of something bigger.

If possible, link those values to current events—to some news story that shows them at work (or failing to work)—to demonstrate their undying relevance.

Historical Precedent

When have others had the feelings, thoughts, and ideas that you and the audience are now sharing?

If there's one thing that binds us all together, it's the fact that we're very bullish on the future of Wisconsin. But we're just continuing a long tradition of optimism—a tradition that began even before there was a State of Wisconsin. In his message to the territorial legislature, our state's first governor said:

> No country has ever been settled by more enterprising, intelligent, and industrious citizens. With such a population, Wisconsin will assume her station as a member of the Union with a character which must entitle her to importance and respect.

> How right he was! And today, as we look forward to the 21st century, we can be just as optimistic as Thomas Flanagan was 175 years ago.

Ending the Acceptance Speech

Invoke the deity. It's OK to wind up by calling on God, especially for humanitarian and charitable awards (if it fits with your personal ideology).

> Thank you once again for your kind words and good wishes . . . and God bless you all.

Thank 'em again—and accept with some positive emotion. Hope is always good: what do you hope for as the awarding organization and its cause go forward?

> Let me close by thanking you once again for this award. I accept it with the hope that someday brotherhood and sisterhood will need no publicity . . . that someday a "humanitarian award" will be just as superfluous as an award for getting up each morning.

THE GOLDEN RULE OF
CEREMONIAL SPEECHWRITING

As you've no doubt noticed from my advice, all effective ceremonial speeches have one thing in common: they interpret the event. Yes, it's true, you're there to introduce, dedicate, or accept. But why?

The traditional marriage ceremony begins with "we are gathered together to unite this man and this woman in holy matrimony." It comes right to the point.

Similarly, your ceremonial speeches should leave no doubt as to why you and your audience are gathered together. It should tell the listeners what thoughts and feelings are appropriate to such a gathering. It should leave them with an understanding of the larger meaning of the ceremony. It should interpret the event. If you can do that, your ceremonial speeches will transcend platitudes; they will have real meaning. Your listeners' lives will be different—because they've heard the magic words that you have spoken.

NOTES

1. The information in this section will also work for tributes and testimonials. Just omit the information related to the speaker's topic.

2. The information in this section can also be used for welcoming remarks.

3. Dedication of Integrated Pest Management Greenhouse, EPCOT Center by Thomas D. Ricke, Senior Vice President, Corporate Affairs, Kraft General Foods, Orlando, FL, Mar. 3, 1992.

7 Listenability

WHAT MAKES A SPEECH "LISTENABLE"?

We all like to listen to speeches that connect with our experiences, that give us new ideas or information, that arouse our emotions, or that change our view of the world. But even apart from content that people <u>want</u> to listen to, you can also write your speech so that your audience will find it <u>easy</u> to listen to. You do this by taking every opportunity to improve its *clarity, closure, coherence,* and *rhythm.*

EDITING FOR CLARITY

A speech has clarity if every sentence is arranged so that it has only one, easily discernible meaning. There's nothing that confuses or misleads the listeners as they mentally process first the earlier, then the later parts of the sentence and arrive at the meaning of the whole.

Since the number of sentences you can write is infinite, there's nothing I can tell you that will cover all the possibilities, unless it's this: Try to BECOME YOUR AUDIENCE.

If you can somehow lose your intimate involvement with what you've written, if you can perceive it with the dispassionate eye or ear of your listener, who has little or no idea of what you're trying to say, then you're well on the way towards achieving clarity.

So put some distance between yourself and your text. There really is a sort of mental detachment that sets in when you toss your script into a drawer (or leave it on a diskette) for a day or a week, then look at it with a fresh mind that has practically forgotten who wrote it and that has let go of some of your implicit logic, background, and detail—to which your audience, of course, has no access.

To edit for clarity is to go through your script, pretending that someone else wrote it and relentlessly examining each sentence for unmistakable, crystalline clarity of meaning. As you do, employ the following seven strategies.

Clarity Strategy #1: Establish a clear connection between pronouns and the words or phrases they refer to.

Pronouns such as *he, she, it,* and *they* are like wild cards, because their meaning is variable; it depends on some other word elsewhere in the sentence. But where? Well, there are two possibilities:

1   The closest possible word, as in "The Americans blame the Russians for the stalemate; *they* blame the Americans." [*They* refers to "the Russians," not to "the Americans."]
2. The word in the same sentence-position, as in "The various divestments saved the company money and earned *it* more than $250 million in cash." [*It* refers to the company, not the money.]

Your task here is to see that the meaning of each wild card is clear. You must make sure that you haven't written a sentence in which the audience can use both interpretation strategies to tell what the wild card refers to.

Here's an example of a sentence that's vague because its structure sends two signals of wild-card meaning.

We are very proud of our progress in quality, and we consider *it* one of our key success criteria.

Which one is the key success criterion—progress or quality? If the listeners are thinking "closest word," *it* refers to "quality." But if they're thinking "same sentence position," *it* refers to "progress."

To fix the ambiguity, skip the pronoun; instead, use the word that signals your intended meaning:

We are very proud of our progress in quality, and we consider quality (or progress) to be one of our key success criteria.

Clarity Strategy #2: Avoid vagueness created by meaningless, impersonal *it*.

In many cases, *it* isn't a wild card (with variable meaning), but only a meaningless place-taker:

It's time to go to lunch.

It's obvious that we need a conference.

Clarity problems may arise when this meaningless *it* occurs in the latter part of the sentence, thus prompting the reader to link it to something that came earlier:

The reorganization wasn't easy, but *it* was considered appropriate that we go forward.

Your listeners will get all the way to *that* before they discover that *it* doesn't refer to "the reorganization" and that "going forward," not "the reorganization," was what was considered appropriate.

To improve clarity, make the sentence personal by telling the audience who did the considering:

The reorganization wasn't easy, but we [or management] considered it appropriate that we go forward.

Clarity Strategy #3: Establish a clear connection between *this* and the word or phrase it refers to.

This is a pointing-word. It's typically used at the beginning of a sentence, where it points back to the entire preceding sentence. This usage is common in conversational speech—so much so, in fact, that the inexperienced speechwriter strings sentences together with *this* and leaves the audience to figure out the connection.

In the example below, *this* refers (somewhat vaguely) to a preceding sentence-idea.

Operators who look at the screen or at any close work for long periods may slow their blink rate. *This* reduces eye lubrication and may be especially uncomfortable for contact lens wearers.

What is it that reduces eye lubrication? Is it the blink rate? Well, after a little head-scratching, we can figure out (on the basis of context—that is, what we know about the world) that the most likely answer is that it's the fact that operators slow their blink rate.

As you edit for clarity, look at each *this* you've put at the beginning of a sentence. If it refers to a whole preceding sentence-idea, make sure the connection is unmistakable. If it isn't, employ one of three fixes:

Fix #1: In "cause-and-effect" sentences, use *thus*.

. . . may slow their blink rate, *thus* reducing . . .

... may slow their blink rate; they *thus* reduce ...

Fix #2: Add a word or phrase after this so that the audience knows what *this* is pointing to.

This *slowing of the blink rate* reduces eye lubrication ...

This *process* reduces ...

Fix #3: Replace *this* with a connecting expression that captures the relationship between the two sentences (this fix may require major renovation in the rest of the sentence—note underlined words).

As a result, eye lubrication is reduced, and contact lens wearers may experience discomfort.

Clarity Strategy #4: Make sure that each "mini-sentence" has the same point of view as the core sentence to which it's attached.

A mini-sentence is a reduced sentence (the person or thing performing the action is usually omitted) tacked on to a whole (or "core") sentence. Often the element missing from the mini-sentence is an implied *you/one/someone*. The audience tries to interpret the mini-sentence by supplying its missing element from the core sentence, so clarity problems arise if the mini- and core sentences have different points of view.

In the following example, the mini-sentence and core sentence have different points of view.

By following these simple procedures, the use of the automatic teller machine will be quick and easy.

The mini-sentence is everything up to the comma; the core sentence is the rest. Now, who's following the proce-

dures? Your listeners have to wait until you get to the core
sentence before they get a clue. They hear *the use,* they think,
"The use is following the procedures? Huh???"—and they
have to recall and reprocess the sentence to get the correct
interpretation.

To avoid this kind of confusion, apply Strategy #4. If the
missing item is an implied *you/one/someone,* put it into the
core sentence:

> By following these simple procedures, *you* can use the
> automatic teller machine quickly and easily.

Now the core and mini-sentences have the same point of
view: YOU are the one following procedures, and YOU are
the one using the machines.

If core and mini-sentences have different points of view,
spell them out:

> If *you* follow these simple procedures, *the use* of the
> automatic teller machine will be quick and easy.

In the following example (from a memo I once received),
the mini-sentence and core sentence have different points of
view.

> May I see the article prior to going to the Vice
> President's office?

Here the mini-sentence—*going to the vice president's office*—
is at the end, but again, we have a clash with the core sentence, in which the point of view is "I," which the reader
then uses in trying to understand the mini-sentence. But it's
not "I" (that is, the writer of the memo) who's going to the
VP's office—it's the article (I know that only because I know
the context).

Again, if core and mini-sentences have different points of view, spell them out:

May *I* see the article before *it* goes to the VP's office?

Clarity Strategy #5: Put *who/which/that* and their associated words as close as possible to the word about which they supply information.

You'll create clarity problems if you keep them separate, as in this example.

Mr. Campbell, a biographer of James Baldwin who grew up in Glasgow . . .

Who grew up in Glasgow—Mr. Campbell or James Baldwin? Our knowledge of the world tells us it must be Campbell, although the sentence structure says "Baldwin."

A revised version, following Clarity Strategy #5, is

Mr. Campbell, a James Baldwin biographer who grew up in Glasgow . . .

Strategy #5 also applies to words that supply information about other words, even when the *who/which/that* doesn't appear, as in

We plan to complete long-term strategic assessments for each of the company's major businesses *linking [= "that link"]* our growth objectives with available capacity.

What is it that links objectives with capacity? The sentence structure says it's "the company's major businesses," but that doesn't make sense. It's got to be the "long-term strategic assessments."

To improve clarity, rearrange the sentence to put information-supplying words as close as possible to the words about which they supply information:

For each of the company's major businesses, we plan to complete long-term *assessments linking* our growth objectives with available capacity.

We plan to complete, for each of the company's major businesses, long-term *assessments linking* our growth objectives with available capacity.

Clarity Strategy #6: Make sure that each item in a series is clearly linked to its "series starter."

And, but, and *or* can create clarity problems because they connect something that comes before with something that comes later. As with *he/she/it,* you're asking the audience to match two items that aren't necessarily right next to each other. So you have to make sure that you haven't stuck in anything that could mistakenly be linked with some other, earlier item.

As you edit and rewrite your script, look for places where you've listed a series of items or events. Here's an example.

The system (i) tracks and reports (A) response time, (B) status of service requests, and (ii) alerts management to unusual circumstances.

Here we have two series starters:

1. *the system* (series: the two things the system does—[i] tracks and reports and [ii] alerts management); and
2. *tracks and reports* (series: the two things that are tracked and reported—[A] response time and [B] status of service).

The clarity problem arises because the writer has linked them all with the second *and*, even though *alerts* belongs to the first series (things the system does).

To fix this sentence, I would add *and* to create clear matches of series items with series starters:

> The system (i) tracks and reports (A) response time and (B) the status of service requests, *and* it (ii) alerts management to unusual circumstances.

Clarity Strategy #7: Eliminate multiple meanings.

Our last stop on the road to clarity is the unintended multiple meaning, the accidental secondary interpretation that arises from words that you've put side by side. This can give a whole different meaning to your sentence.

It's true that your listeners can usually guess your intent on the basis of text and context. So your potential ambiguities will rarely confuse them completely. But if total listenability is what you're after, you want to avoid even the slightest disruption of your audience's attention.

As before, since the number of different sentences is practically infinite, the best way to root out ambiguity is to get some detachment from your speech text, so that you approximate the distance from which your audience approaches it. Then proceed, on a case-by-case basis, to look for double meanings. Here are some places where they typically lurk.

Double-Meaning Possibility #1: Items linked by *and, but, or*

If the link-up of a series starter with an unintended item actually makes sense (sort of), then a real double meaning can result. This one comes from an article praising a conscientious nurse:

She has tended infants and broken bones at local hospitals.

Amazing! She's Florence Nightingale in the Maternity Ward, but over in Physical Therapy, she turns into Attila the Hun.

The double meaning arises from the fact that the word *and* could be interpreted as linking either *infants* and *bones* (that's the intended meaning: She's tended (1) infants and (2) broken bones) or *tended* and *broken* (in which case she breaks bones). To fix, add a word similar to *tended* so that you create two distinct groups around *and*:

She has [tended infants] and [*treated* broken bones] at local hospitals.

At this point, if you're tempted to think, "Well, I really could have figured that out. No nurse goes around breaking bones"—DON'T.

It's true that much communication is so poor that we come to expect that we'll have to work to get the message. But speechwriting is communication, not puzzle-construction. The whole point of making your speech listenable is to minimize the effort required of the audience. And the less attention and intellectual effort your listeners must spend on deciphering your intended meaning, the more they'll have for understanding the message itself.

Double-Meaning Possibility #2: Misplaced time and place expressions

Consider the following:

The Board decided to fire the CEO in New York.

Does this mean that the Board made the decision in New

York—or that in some other city, they decided to do the deed in their Manhattan offices?

Writers often put time and place expressions at the end because they think of them last. But that placement doesn't always yield a clear, one-meaning sentence.

I always try to move time and place expressions to the beginning (that's a more natural place for them anyway, since they set the stage for the rest of the sentence):

In New York, the Board decided to fire the CEO.

Or—to signal the other meaning—

The Board decided that in New York it would fire the CEO.

Double-Meaning Possibility #3: -er (= "more") words with than

More and all the *-er* words that have a "more" meaning (*faster, cleaner, sooner,* etc.) make up another class of linking expression; the message is always that "item A is '-er than' item B." And as in other, similar cases, your task is to see that the correct match-up is not disturbed by words that come between the essential elements, as in this example.

Pregnant women dream about animals more than other women.

Two meanings are possible: (1) they dream about animals more than they dream about other women, and (2) they dream about animals more frequently than other women do. To fix, insert extra words to spell out the intended meaning, as I just did in (1) and (2).

Another possibility is to keep the "A is -er than B" pattern together and move other, associated words to the right:

Pregnant women dream more than other women about animals.

Double-Meaning Possibility #4: *Both . . . and* with an *-(e)s* word (i.e., a plural) after *both*

The problem here is simply that *both* followed by a plural can mean "the two," as in "Both employees and managers attended the meeting." Two employees? Or employees as well as managers? If it's the latter, use *as well as*:

Employees *as well as* managers attended the meeting.

Double-Meaning Possibility #5: Multiple word meanings

Clarity means that each word in your document can have only its intended meaning. The person who wrote

These data will be used for specific executions.

most likely did not mean that we're going to use the data to tell us whom we're going to line up before a firing squad, but rather that we're using the data to tell us how we're going to put specific strategies into practice. And sure, audiences will know that because they live in a world in which business people don't kill each other (not literally, at least). But they'll have an unintended and unnecessary chuckle—at the writer's expense.

Don't give them that opportunity. Check your script for words that might have other, unintended meanings, and make substitutions where necessary.

Also, read your text aloud, so that you can hear words that sound like other words. The phrase "the humorist Dave Barry" is clear enough on the page, but when said aloud, it sounds an awful lot like "the humorous Dave Barry." Revise to "Dave Barry, the humor writer."

EDITING FOR CLOSURE

The second way you can make your speech more listenable is to improve closure.

Because communication is received linearly, listeners not only process the structure of the early part of a sentence; they also form hunches about the structure of the rest of the sentence, well before they actually get to the end. You can help them do this by setting up expectations about how the sentence will go—and then by fulfilling them.

Your text has closure if its sentences, wherever possible, are written in such a way as to set up and fulfill expectations. The first part gives the reader a clue about how the whole thing is going to turn out, and then the sentence does in fact turn out in exactly that way.

Here are your strategies for improving closure.

Closure Strategy #1: Move time and place expressions to the front.

This is pretty self-explanatory. The reason, as I said earlier, is that by doing so, you set the stage for the rest; the audience knows that the remainder of the sentence will tell what happens within that particular setting. (An additional benefit: clarity. By moving the time/place expression to the front, you avoid the confusion that might come from the audience's incorrectly associating it with some item that comes later.)

Closure Strategy #2: Put the items of series in their natural (real-world) order.

An example of unnatural ordering is

> We plan to excel in distribution, manufacturing, and marketing.

Natural ordering would be

. . . manufacturing, marketing, and distribution.

The same principle applies to the ordering of events. In this example

Moreover, the adverse effects on our trade position from last year's severe overvaluation of the dollar must be expected to extend well into and even through 1983.

the writer mentions the effects, then their cause (severe overevaluation). I would revise to put the cause first:

Moreover, the dollar was severely overvalued last year, and we must expect that the adverse effects on our trade position will extend well into 1983 and even through the year.

Closure Strategy #3: Make sure that each word in a series is in the same form.

In this example, series items are in different forms:

If you have any thoughts along these lines, we would appreciate *hearing from you* during the conference or *a brief memo* to Frank Jones at National Headquarters.

It's not hard to see the speaker's logic: he/she would like either (1) to hear from us or (2) to receive a brief memo. But when the sentence is assembled in this way, it throws us off track.

To improve closure, put series items in the same form:

If you have any thoughts along these lines, we would appreciate (1) *hearing from you* during the conference or

(2) *receiving a brief memo* addressed to Frank Jones at National Headquarters.

Also—and this is very important—make sure that each word in the series is in the form required by the accompanying words. If two <u>different</u> forms of the <u>same</u> word are required, you cannot omit one of them, as in

> However, a second and equally important focus *has and continues to be* directed toward the design of inherently maintainable products.

> Dramatic changes are taking place in the way service organizations *are and will deliver* their services.

You can set up your sentences in this manner <u>only</u> when the <u>same</u> form of *deliver* is required in both parts of the series (e.g., "Service organizations *can and must deliver* services more efficiently.")—but not in the two cases above. You need to use different forms of the same word, as required by the accompanying words:

> However, a second and equally important focus *has been and continues to be* directed toward the design of inherently maintainable products.

> Dramatic changes are taking place in the way service organizations *are delivering and will deliver* their services.

Closure Strategy #4: Use up-front signals.

Our language has a number of two-part expressions that set up and fulfill expectations.

> Not only . . . but also . . .
> If . . . then . . .
> Although/Even though . . . nevertheless,/still,

(N)either . . . (n)or . . .

Both . . . and . . .

On the one hand, . . . On the other (hand), . . .

If we hear a *not only*, we know that a *but also* is coming; the first two words have given us a powerful clue about the rest of the sentence.

You can also use <u>one</u>-word signals to set up the first part of a two-part sentence and achieve the same effect, as in

> *When* our employees learn the details of the new compensation plan, they'll be very pleased.

As soon as we hear the *when*, we have a good idea about how the rest of the sentence will go. We know that the speaker is about to put two events in a time sequence, so we mentally supply a *then* before the second half ("then they'll be very pleased").

The same principle applies to

> *Because/Since* the competition has introduced a new product, we must accelerate our own product development program.

Again, the first word creates an expectation for the rest of the sentence: we expect a cause-and-effect relationship between two events, and we mentally supply a *therefore* before the *we must accelerate*.

Since these up-front signals are so critical to effective closure (and thus to listenability), you should use them whenever you have a chance. And you have many more chances than you might think.

To discover these opportunities, try to get a sense of the overall meaning of the sentence. If there's any hint of the following meanings, the sentence is a candidate for rearrangement into a version with an up-front signal.

Sentence meaning	Up-front signal
time sequence	use *When* . . . or *After* . . .
cause-effect	use *Because* . . . or *Since* . . .
if X, then Y	use words in left-hand column
given this, *then* that	use words in left-hand column
although/even though X, *nevertheless/not necessarily* Y	use words in left-hand column
regardless of X/*despite* X, *nevertheless,* Y	use words in left-hand column

Very often the verb (the word that expresses action or tells you what's going on in the sentence) will give you the hint you need, as in

> Statements of the potential economic effects of events, without regard to their relative probability cannot *lead* to the identification of those security exposures that are worthy of corrective action and those which are not.

Lead to—now there's an "if-then"meaning if I ever saw one! So just start with *If* and let the rest follow naturally:

> *If* we (simply, merely) state the potential economic effects of events, without regard to their relative probability, (*then*) we cannot identify those security exposures . . .

Closure Strategy #5: Avoid front-loading.

Your listeners must remember the early part of each sentence so that they can put it together with the later part. So you don't want to let your sentence-beginnings get too long and complex.

Here's an example of a front-loaded sentence:

> It is no secret that an alarming percentage of attempts to contact people during normal business hours by phone fail.

To understand this sentence, the audience has to remember everything up to the last word. And that's really asking too much.

If you find that your script contains a front-loaded sentence, try to break it into two parts, each a sentence in itself; if possible, introduce the first with an up-front signal. As above, start by getting a sense of the overall meaning. In the example above, the "secret" part is really a secondary idea; what we really have is a "when . . . then" relationship—something like *"when* people try to call each other . . . (*then/that's when*) they fail."

Break up front-loaded sentences into self-contained sentences; use up-front signals if possible.

It is no secret that in an alarming number of cases, *when* (**SENTENCE:** people try to contact each other by phone during normal business hours), they fail.

Closure Strategy #6: Move the important item to the end.

English sentences have an inherent rhythmic pattern: other things being equal, the strongest "beat" in the sentence is at the end. You can give your sentences a nice, satisfying sense of closure by putting the item you want to emphasize as close as possible to the end, thus fulfilling your audience's expectations—and improving listenability.

Weak closure:

Since software is written for a particular operating system, it is advantageous to minimize the number of different operating systems.

Important item moved to end:

Since software is written for a particular operating system, it is advantageous to keep the number of different operating systems to a *minimum.*

"Operating systems" isn't the key idea in the second part; we've already mentioned that. "Minimize" is. The second version puts the key idea where it belongs. Read the two aloud, and you'll hear the difference.

EDITING FOR COHERENCE

The third aspect of listenability is *coherence.* The more coherent your text, the more listenable your speech will be.

Your speech has coherence if the relationship between successive sentences, paragraphs, and sections is unmistakably clear to the audience. Coherence, in other words, is what unites the components of a text into larger elements: sentences into paragraphs, paragraphs into sections, sections into the whole speech.

As you edit, employ the following two strategies to make your writing more coherent.

Coherence Strategy #1: Use signposts.

Whether you script out your speech or merely provide yourself with an outline or notes, you'll want to make liberal use of "signposts"—words and phrases that signal relationships between pieces of your text. The more consistently you use them, the clearer those relationships will be.

Signposts are especially important in oral presentations: since your listeners can't flip pages to go back and refresh their memories, they must constantly be kept abreast of the structure and development of your talk.

Here are some examples. If one of these (or some other; you can easily expand each list) seems to clearly express a relationship between one piece and the next, use it. Remember that your listeners don't know where you're going; you have to show them the way.

Sentence-to-sentence signposts

then/later/subsequently

consequently/as a result/so

nevertheless/still/even so

moreover/and/also/furthermore/in addition

on the other hand

(and) yet

on the contrary

but/however

for example/for instance

in other words/that is

in fact

The last three can routinely be omitted. According to the conventions of English, the absence of a sentence signpost typically means "for example," "in other words," or "in fact."

Paragraph-to-paragraph (and sentence-to-sentence) signposts

in the first place/to begin with

second/third/fourth . . . next

finally/last (of all)

another reason/factor/disadvantage/consequence/ benefit/result/element/problem.[1]

Section-to-section (and paragraph-to-paragraph) signposts

We've/I've been discussing X. Next we'll/I'll consider Y.

Now let me/let's turn to

All of these facts have a very simple explanation.

This is the problem/cause/disadvantage/(etc., depending on your organizational plan)

What might the solution/effects/benefits/(etc., depending on your plan) be?

One more comment on signposts: As a rule, the more significant the boundary, the more prominent the signpost should be. Intersentence signposts are only a word or two long, while signposts that separate sections can be as long as a couple of sentences, for example, "Well, there you have a fairly complete account of how we got to where we are. Now let me spend the rest of my time talking about where we go from here." You might even summarize the speech so far:

> Well, I hope you now have a better understanding of the people you're trying to reach with your advertising and your products.
>   To sum it up . . . they have a lot more food choices, and they're a lot more adventurous. They're time-starved, stressed out, and not inclined to spend a lot of time cooking. They're buying food products in places other than traditional supermarkets, and they're buying a lot more prepared foods. They're still concerned about healthful food choices, but they're becoming less rigid and focusing more on the positives. They're using food as a way to be nice to themselves. They're very much concerned with value. And they're getting older, eating some of the same foods, but requiring changes in others.
>   So far, I've surveyed the terrain on which you must build your bridge to excellence. Now let me turn to

the strategies that I think will get your bridge built. Given the conditions I've outlined, there are three of them, three keys to success.[2]

Coherence Strategy #2: Link one sentence to another by repeating a word (or idea) and/or by pointing with *this*.

If you carry over an idea from one sentence to the next, a powerful way to impart coherence is to use, in the second of two sentences, a word or phrase that repeats an idea in the first (I've done that consistently throughout this book, so you don't have to look far for examples). If you use *this* with the repeated word, you can link sentences *and* point back to an element in the previous sentence. Or you can simply point by using *this* alone—but make sure it's not vague (see Clarity Strategy #3).

YOU'VE GOT RHYTHM

The final piece of listenability is the skillful use of prose rhythms.

You thought only poetry had rhythm? Not so! Some poems have a regular rhythmic pattern throughout. But in a great deal of modern poetry, and in prose as well, rhythm is the result of the writer's arranging words so as to take advantage of the natural "beat" of the language over shorter stretches of speech.

The term for perceived loudness of one syllable relative to another is *stress*. (I say "perceived" because it's not always clear that stressed syllables are really louder.)

In some languages, stress is predictable; it always falls on the same syllable of the word. But not in English, where stress is "free." Some syllables sound louder than others. But which ones? That depends on both the structure of the word and on the sounds it contains. Also, there are different degrees of word-stress (*colonization* has at least four), and all of those are amplified or suppressed according to the emphasis in the sentence as a whole.

So your first step in understanding prose rhythms is to sharpen your awareness of all these weaker and stronger beats, by listening for the many different degrees of emphasis that fall on the various syllables of the words in a sentence.

One other piece of background. The natural sentence-accentuation of English places one major stress at or near the beginning and another as close as possible to the end—which usually means the stressed syllable of the last "content" word (noun, verb, etc.) rather than the last preposition or other "structure" words. You can hear this quite clearly if you recite a simple list, which has no internal meaning:

> MONday, Tuesday, Wednesday, Thursday, Friday, SATurday

Enough theory. First practical application: Be alert to cases in which a single stress pattern sends two meanings. Does "She wasn't responsible" mean that she couldn't be counted on—or that she couldn't be blamed? Revise to "She was irresponsible" or "She wasn't the one who was responsible."

Next, use that sentence-stress pattern so that sound reinforces meaning. As Dwight Bolinger points out, "since we depend on stress to highlight the most important and informative idea in the sentence, the trick is to arrange our words so that the one signifying that idea will come at that point"— in other words, the last content word before a major break.[3]

Note the difference between

Weak emphasis: This expansion is beginning to look like one that could be of long duration and with more strength than has been the conventional expectation in recent weeks.

Stressed emphasis: This expansion is beginning to look as if it will be longer than has been conventionally expected in recent weeks—and stronger as well.

(Also note that the revised version uses rhyme for emphasis.)

Another way to make sound reinforce meaning is to use short sentences when you're writing about quick, brief events:

Our business is fast-paced in almost any way you can think of. Product life-cycles are short. Companies rise— and sometimes fall—with spectacular speed. Price/performance is a steeply declining curve.

Another pointer: be sensitive to jingling rhythms and unintentional rhymes that distract listeners (e.g., "The relaxation of the limitations on the regulation of transportation."). Typically responsible for this effect are the *-ation/-ition* suffixes that are so frequent in business and technical communication.

But even as you eliminate the distracting rhythms, you can consciously employ others, particularly at the ends of sentences that conclude important thought sequences. Read this next example aloud—

. . . so that as we embark upon what may be the most exciting period of our history, we will do so as a company of diVERsity, PROmise, and STRENGTH.

—and you'll hear the solid "ONE-two-three" (or "dactylic," or "waltz") rhythm of the last three words. Also, the sequence

ends with a word that is strong both accentually and seman-
tically, followed by a rhythmic "rest," in which the listener
mentally supplies the last two "beats."

This next example

> Every assessment of our nation's economic health car-
> ries within it one STARK and TROUBling FACT: . . .

ends with two clear "weak-STRONG" (or "iambic") sequences.
Read it aloud, and you'll hear three strong beats (on *stark,*
troub-, and *fact*) that rap sharply at the door of the listener's
attention.

Here's another:

> And the third risk: data that is OBsolete, INcomplete, or
> JUST PLAIN WRONG.

Here, two rhyming "weak-weak-STRONG" sequences are
followed by three single beats on the last three words. Notice
how the natural sentence-accent falls right where it should—
on the emphasized word *wrong.*

There's one more way to make your speechwriting sound
like natural speech. This is not a special effect like the others.
It's a basic strategy that you want to employ in every sentence, deviating from it only for good reason.

When we talk, we never crowd too much verbiage
between major grammatical breaks. That has something to do
with the limitations on our language-producing ability—and
probably with our listeners' language-processing abilities as
well. The length of these grammatical chunks can vary: Some
speakers are extraordinarily fluent, while others can't articu-
late three words without a *like* or an *I mean* or a *y'know.* But

for most of us, the words between pauses contain only two to five major stresses:

So EVen SMALLer COMpanies /can BUY DAta /PUT it into a MIcrocomputer/ aLONG with their inTERnal inforMAtion /and ACcess it EASily and inexPENsively.

As you fine-tune your speech, look for places where you've put too many word-stresses between pauses, and regroup accordingly.

Also, be sure you haven't carried any grammatical constructions across pauses. You don't want to pile up words between pauses and put rhythm and meaning out of joint, as in this example:

The battle against inflation / is closer to victory / than a year ago / most of us would have dared hope.

By putting "than a year ago" right after "victory," the writer leads us to think that the two are linked—that we're closer to victory than we were a year ago—when it's really our hopes of a year ago that he/she is talking about.

Here's the revision:

The battle against inflation / is closer to victory / than most of us would have dared hope / only a year ago.

Notice how I've brought related groups of words (i.e., *a year ago* and *dared hope)* into alignment with natural speech rhythms.

Write your speeches according to the principles in this chapter (and use the personal style—see next chapter—everywhere it's appropriate), and you really will be "writing for the ear." Your speech will sound conversational and be easy and pleasant to listen to.

NOTES

1. Here I'm simply reminding you to use as signposts the very same words that you use to remind the audience of your organizational plan(s); see Chapter 2.

2. "Building the Bridge to Excellence." Keynote remarks by Robert Eckert to the National Turkey Federation, San Francisco, CA, Jan. 13, 1997.

3. Dwight Bolinger, *Aspects of Language* (New York: Harcourt Brace Jovanovich), p. 602.

Style: Dressing for the Occasion

THE IMPORTANCE OF STYLE

How many times have you heard, "It's not what you said—it's the way you said it"? Inappropriate style can seriously undermine the effectiveness of your message. You wouldn't start a sympathy note by writing, "Too bad your old man croaked." And you wouldn't begin a letter to your brother like this:

Dear Elliot:

Your correspondence of the 18th has been received and reviewed by our family, and congratulations are herewith offered.

What's wrong? The problem is not what was said, but how it was said. In both cases, the phrasing and word choice are totally inappropriate—too folksy in the first example, too stuffy in the second.

When you write your speech script, you want to do it in a style that's appropriate to your audience, subject, and situation. In the next chapter, we'll get into word choice; for the moment, let's concentrate on the grammatical options that account for style.

PERSONAL VERSUS IMPERSONAL STYLE

I'm going to show you two writing styles that represent polar opposites; as we'll see, there are also a great many possibilities in between. One extreme is the **personal (or "P")** style; this is the language of communication between familiars or equals. The other is the **impersonal (or "I")** style, the language of power and authority.

The personal style is informal. It's the language of memos, notes, letters, and other communication between people who know each other well and are not writing for a wider audience. It's also the language of those forms of communication that seek to create the impression of informality—for example, newspaper columns, advertising copy (which relies heavily on a false familiarity with the audience), and most of the speeches you'll write.

The impersonal style is formal. It's the language of most scholarly and academic writing, of most business letters, memos, proposals and reports, and of laws, contracts, covenants, warranties, rituals, proclamations, and other official communications.

The personal style is individual and private. It's the language of people speaking for themselves. It allows the writer to use favorite expressions to express his/her personality.

The impersonal style is institutional and public. It gives little or no hint of the person behind it, which is why it's appropriate for communication by institutions (businesses, government, universities, nonprofit agencies, committees, organizations, and so on) or by people speaking for institutions.

The personal style is conversational. It sounds like everyday speech, but without the false starts, the "I mean"s, the "you know"s, and other flaws that we hear in impromptu conversation.

The impersonal style is <u>professional</u>. It sounds businesslike, dignified, or scholarly.

Although most of your speeches will be in the personal style, there may be times when you want to be more impersonal. You can write in either style, or a mix of both, by following a few simple principles, which I'll show you. Each principle represents a choice that you make whenever a particular opportunity occurs. <u>What</u> you say doesn't change—it's all in <u>how</u> you say it.

Style-Choice Principle #1: For the personal style, choose expressions of ACTION; for the impersonal style, choose ABSTRACTION.

The impersonal style is full of words that denote abstract processes and events; you can recognize them by their endings. A great many of them end in *-tion*, *-ing*, *-ity*, or *-ness*. Once you can recognize the larger, more familiar classes of abstract words, you'll find it easy to see the pattern into which they all fall.

Examples of abstract expressions
expansion of IRAs
production of automobiles
growth of the business
hatred of vegetables

The idea behind Principle #1 is that these expressions can almost always be interchanged with action-expressions that have the same meaning but are more personal in style because when you use an action-expression you typically have to spell out <u>who's doing</u> the action.

To go from impersonal (I) to personal (P)
Just convert the abstraction to action and supply a word or words for whoever is performing the action. Once you

have that much, rearrange the rest of the sentence to fit. You'll generally wind up with a little sentence inside your sentence (I've put them in curly brackets below).

To go from personal (P) to impersonal (I)

Reverse the process; remove the actor, change action to abstraction—and adjust the rest of the sentence accordingly.

I (abstraction)   The *modernization* of our facilities is proceeding on schedule.

P (action)   {*We're modernizing* our facilities} [add: and] proceeding on schedule.

I (abstraction)   Current *projections* show a very constrained outlook.

P (action)   {*We are/Our staff* is currently *projecting*} a very constrained outlook.

I (abstraction)   Management recommended *radical cost reductions.*

P (action)   Management recommended [add: that] {*we cut* our costs radically}.

Occasionally, you create the personal expression by grabbing the action word from the larger sentence:

I (abstraction)   The *modernization* of our facilities *has begun.*

P (action)   {*We've begun to modernize*} our facilities.

If your abstract expression is at the beginning, you can often convert to the personal style by starting with *if, when,* or *since.* As we saw in the last chapter (Closure Strategy #4), you can identify such sentences from the meaning of the verb, as in the first example in which *require,* which means that "A demands B," suggests that you might be able to rewrite with *if A . . . then B.*

I (abstraction)	*Living* within our means will require *facing up to* . . . [1]
P (action)	*If* {we're going to live within our means}, [then] {*we'll (have to) face up to* . . . }
I (abstraction)	Any *increase* in the gasoline tax of sufficient size to significantly impact the budget deficit . . .
P (action)	If {*we/the government increase(s)* the gasoline tax} enough to significantly impact the budget deficit . . .

When you go to the personal style in this way, you get the added benefit of better closure via the up-front signal *if,* which sets up expectations of a two-part sentence and thus gives the audience, early on in the sentence, a strong clue about how the whole thing is going to go (again, see Closure Strategy #4).

Style-Choice Principle #2: For the personal style, choose "doing" expressions; for the impersonal style, choose "done-to" expressions.[2]

As with Principle #1, when you convert from impersonal to personal, you have to say who's performing the action, thus making the "P" style personal. On the other hand, if the person (or group or entity) performing the action is unknown or irrelevant—perhaps because the audience already knows who or what it is—then the "done-to," impersonal expression will do the trick.

I (done-to)	Three thousand additional employees *were hired.*
P (doing)	*We* (or *The firm,* etc.) *hired* three thousand additional employees.

I (done-to)	Our cost reduction efforts *were intensified.*
P (doing)	*We intensified* our cost-reduction efforts.
I (done-to)	Consider the following specifics, which *were drawn* from that study.
P (doing)	Consider the following specifics, which *I* (or *we, our consultants,* etc.) *drew* from that study.

A special case: stripped-down "done-to" expression. Sometimes you don't find the "done-to" construction in its full form; there may be only one word with the "done-to" meaning:

I (done-to)	When *combined* with renewed emphasis on product quality, such efforts can . . .

This is really an abbreviated form of *they* (i.e., the efforts) *are combined.* All you do here is change *are combined* to a "doing" expression and supply the missing element—the doer of the action—as before:

P (doing)	When *we combine them* with renewed emphasis on product quality, such efforts can . . .

Another special case: "done-to" expressions with impersonal *it.* Many sentences that begin with a meaningless, impersonal *it* contain a "done-to" expression and can thus be converted to the personal style. Just change the "done to" part to "doing" and replace the *it* with whoever's doing the action.

I (done-to)	*It is assumed* that new products will claim a significant market share.
P (doing)	*We/I/Marketing Staff/*(etc.) *assume(s)* that the new products will claim a significant market share.

I (done-to)   *It is intended* that these funds be used for
                   R&D.
P (doing)   *We/I/The Finance Committee/*(etc.) *intend(s)*
                   that these funds be used for R&D.

Style-Choice Principle #3: For the personal style, break up long compound words; for the impersonal style, keep them.

Our language has thousands of compound words with two members—*house plant, school book, driver training, cat food,* and so on. To know what each of these compounds means, we need to know (1) the meanings of the individual words, and (2) the relationship between those elements (cat food is food FOR cats; a house plant is a plant IN a house).

The writers of technical, legal, scholarly, and other specialized communications like to string words together to create new, longer compounds; to understand these the reader must mentally rearrange the elements and reconstruct the implied relationships:

gasoline tax increase = increase IN the tax ON gasoline

user call placement procedure = procedure BY WHICH users place calls

board meeting agenda = agenda FOR the meeting OF the board

The impersonal style is full of these strings; compounds of three, four, or more members are not unusual. One reason is that for specialists communicating with each other, long compounds become a kind of in-group shorthand. Speakers and writers don't have to spell them out, because the audience already knows what they mean. In the official language of

institutions, their purpose is less functional and more orna-
mental: people use them because they make communication
sound more impersonal (and perhaps, by association with scientific and technical writing, more "professional" or "precise").

The personal style, on the other hand, is like spontaneous
speech. It uses only those compounds that are clearly under-
standable; in other words, audiences already know the
relationships between the parts and thus regard them as single words, as with *house plant* and *cat food*. All the rest are
broken up and rearranged, with their relationships spelled
out.

**Style-Choice Principle #4: For the personal style,
break up two-part *who-* and *which*-phrases that
express location, direction, or connection and put the
location/direction/connection word at the end; for
the impersonal style, keep the two items together.**

This may sound a little complicated, but a couple of examples
will show you that I'm referring to some very common constructions.[3]

I: *At whom* was she laughing?
P: *Who* was she laughing *at*?

After the location/direction/connection word (in this case,
at), always use *whom*, not *who*.

I: This is another area *with which* we are familiar.
P: This is another area (*which*)/(*that*) we are familiar *with*.
I: The company encountered competition *for which* it had
     not planned.
P: The company encountered competition (*which*) it had not
     planned *for*.

When there's no mention of anybody performing the action, the personal version drops the *which* entirely:

I: Chicago is a great city *in which* to do business.
P: Chicago is a great city to do business *in*.

There are two exceptions. First, when there's a lot of material between the *in/at/*(etc.) + *which* group and the end, don't bother breaking up the group; if the two elements get too far apart, the reader will have trouble remembering the connection between them. Thus:

I and P: Chicago is a great city, *in which* a high-tech entre-
           preneurial company will have little difficulty find-
           ing start-up funds.

The second exception: Principle #4 doesn't apply to time expressions. *Before which, during which,* and *after which* sound OK in either style.

Style-Choice Principle #5: For the personal style, use contractions; for the impersonal style, don't.

These two-word blends are a very strong signal of the personal style. Here are two categories, with my recommendations for usage. Remember, *all* of these are personal forms; the impersonal forms would be uncontracted—*I am, you will,* and so on.

Category 1: Acceptable personal style for all but the most formal/impersonal speeches

■ Contractions with *not: won't, wouldn't, shouldn't, can't, couldn't. Mightn't* and *oughtn't* belong here, too, because they're contractions with *not*. But they sound odd to me. If they sound OK to you, go ahead and use them.

- ▪ Contractions consisting of pronoun or *that* + *am/are/is*: *I'm, you're, he's, she's, it's, we're, they're, that's.*
- ▪ Contractions with *will*: *I'll, you'll, he'll, she'll, we'll, they'll.*
- ▪ Contractions with *have/has*: *I've, you've, he's, she's, it's, they've.*
- ▪ Contraction of *I would*: *I'd.*

Category #2: Acceptable personal style only in the most informal communications

- ▪ Contractions with *is,* e.g., *John's* (as in *"John's* writing the letter"), *manager's* (as in "The *manager's* leaving").
- ▪ Contraction of *it will*: *it'll.*
- ▪ Contraction of pronoun (except *I*) + *would*: *you'd, he'd, she'd, we'd, they'd.*
- ▪ Contractions of pronoun + *had*: *I'd, you'd, he'd, she'd, they'd.*

There are many other contractions in spoken English, and I could've (= could have) named them all if the editor'd (= editor had) asked me to. But those are about all that you'll find—and want to use—in your everyday speechmaking. Save the rest for the dialogue in your novel.

PERSONAL OR IMPERSONAL?
HOW TO CHOOSE YOUR STYLE

While most of your speeches will be in the personal style, some will require a little more formality—for example, a eulogy or a serious business or scientific/technical presentation. Ask yourself (1) how your subject is typically discussed, and (2) what your audience's expectations are—and adjust your language accordingly.

Principles 1 through 5 show you how to make your writing sound like conversational speech: just pick the personal form every time. But sometimes you want your speech to be a little more formal, less chatty. So to create a style that's in between, apply one or more of the principles to get the effect you want (to go from impersonal to personal, start with #5, then add #1, then the others).

POSTSCRIPT ON STYLE: CREATING AN "IMPLIED DIALOGUE"

There's one more way to make your speech sound conversational: incorporate, at various places, (1) your own reactions to what you're saying, and (2) your anticipations of the audience's reactions. Skilled monologists employ these tactics to make their presentations more interactive by involving the audience (if only implicitly)—and so can you.

For examples, see Chapter 12, notes 33, 38, 40, 45, and 51.

NOTES

1. This example has two abstract expressions; I'm converting both to the personal form.

2. "Doing" and "done-to" correspond, respectively, to "active" and "passive." I'm trying to keep the grammatical terminology to a minimum.

3. Again, I'm trying to avoid grammatical terminology. For those of you who do remember your high-school English classes, a translation of Principle #4 is, "In the informal/personal style, it's OK to put the preposition at the end of the sentence."

Word Choice: Finding the Lightning

The difference between the almost right word and the right word is really a large matter—'tis the difference between the lightning-bug and the lightning.

Mark Twain

EDITING FOR WORD CHOICE

Once you have your script in near-final form, it's time to look at each one of the "content" words in your text (that is, the words that actually mean something, as opposed to words like *if*, *but*, and *although*, which tell us what role a word plays in the sentence or what its relationship is to some other word). You might even highlight them so that you can examine them, one by one, in the light of the information in this chapter.

Your objective is to be sure that in each case, you've picked the right word—the word that does exactly what you want it to do, and nothing else.

But what do you want it to do? To answer that question, we have to ask another:

WHAT DO WORDS DO?

When you understand that, you'll have a better grasp of what writers and speakers do when they select one particular word (or phrase) over another.

Words have three functions (and one word can perform all three):

1. **They label.** They refer to (or point to, or symbolize) reality—that is, the world outside of language.
2. **They express judgments.** They convey the writer's feelings about and evaluations of the reality they symbolize.
3. **They express "distance."** They tell the audience whether the writer considers the communication to be public or private, and they signal that writer and audience are members of the same in-group.

Let's look at these functions in more detail. After I explain what each one is, I'll tell you how you do it with the words you choose.

WORD-CHOICE FUNCTION #1: LABELING

How Words Name Things—and why you can't "tell it like it is"

Philosophers, linguists, and psychologists have done a mountain of research about how words symbolize reality, but since practical advice is the point here, I'll skip right to the bottom line: with the possible exception of words that sound like the things they name (e.g., *meow, crash, gurgle*) **there is no necessary connection between a name and a thing.** The only "correct" word for something is the word that people agree to use for that thing. Part of what's involved in knowing a language is being able to match up the world of language (words) with the world of experience (reality) in pretty much the same way as the other speakers of that language do.

On the face of it, that seems pretty simple and clear-cut. But the minute we look at how it actually works in practice, two problems quickly become apparent.

The first labeling problem is that some words we use don't symbolize a reality that everyone will agree to. Thus, words like *God, angel, Satan,* and *reincarnation* may have very powerful and immediate meaning for some people—and none at all for others. We won't be dealing with this problem here, because it has more to do with people's beliefs about what's real and what isn't than with the nature and process of communication.

The second problem is that people disagree about the match-up of labels to things. These disagreements center around the question of what <u>properties</u> the thing has to have before we can properly attach the name to it. It's a problem of classification.

My wife tells me she wants to buy a leather <u>jacket</u>. I envision an outer garment that comes down to the waist—like my own—but she informs me that women's jackets may go down as far as the knees.

If we can have communication problems with everyday items such as jackets, just think what happens when we try to decide what is "moral," "true," "democratic," or "obscene"—when we try to use labels to classify experiences that vary widely and cause strong emotions in us and when we try to get others to agree with our classifications. What happens is that we get a lot of conflict between people, <u>all</u> of whom think they are "telling it like it is."

The fact is that <u>none</u> of us can "tell it like it is" or "call a spade a spade." People who insist that you do that are saying nothing more than "Use a label that <u>I</u> like—and then we'll be friends."

Of course, in the vast majority of cases, people do agree; if they didn't, communication would be even harder than it is. But in a great many other cases, word choice is crucially important. You can say, "We're downsizing the sales force and consolidating our manufacturing operations," or you can say, "We're firing a lot of salespeople and closing some of our plants." There are definite reasons for picking one over the other (actually, I'm not too fond of either one, but sometimes the reality is there, and you have to talk about it somehow).

What "The Dictionary" Does

At this point, you may be wondering whether you can't just go to the dictionary to find out what a word "really means." Sorry, but that's not the way it works. Still, if you understand what a dictionary does, you'll be in a much better position to use it effectively.

In the first place, there's no such thing as "the dictionary." There are dozens of them on the market, and they differ among themselves, as you can readily see if you go to a bookstore and compare two definitions of the same word.

Second, meanings are constantly shifting, so that a later edition of the same dictionary can give you different information.

Third, the labeling process—the attaching of words to classes of things— depends not only on "must have" qualities (*jacket* must refer to a garment for the upper part of the body), but also on those slippery "nice to have" qualities as well (a jacket may or may not be an outer garment; it may reach to the waist [men's outer garment] or to the knees [women's]). Dictionaries do mention and describe these, but that still leaves the boundaries vague—as indeed they are in actual language usage.

Nevertheless, a dictionary is an essential tool for the speechwriter. Think of it as a collection of correspondences or match-ups. It reports—and to some degree decides—what words, as of the date of publication, have equivalent meanings (that is, what words are symbols for the same reality). It also tells you what words have partially equivalent meanings, and it explains the ways in which those meanings overlap.

Summary: Labeling and Classifying

To sum up, then, the symbolic process works like this: words and phrases represent reality in ways that are understood and agreed upon by speakers of a language. That's part of what it means to "know a language." So a writer's decision to use a particular word is in fact a decision to classify a certain piece of reality—to put it in the group that deserves this particular label—on the basis of its characteristics.

Truth or Consequences

Now that you know how words name things, you can see that choosing one word over another is a game of "truth or consequences": if you fail to tell "the truth" as your audience sees it, you suffer the consequences. But if you know your listeners well enough, you can anticipate their reaction—you'll know what labels they're likely to take issue with—and you'll explain and defend your word choices as necessary.

That doesn't necessarily mean you'll devote a sentence or a paragraph to explaining why you used this or that particular word (although that may sometimes be required). Much more often, we anticipate our audience's objections, and we employ little words and phrases that either "hedge" our choice of labels or "push" the audience to accept it.

Anticipating Objections to a Word Choice: "Hedging"

If you think your audience might have a problem with a label you've chosen, you may want to consider using a "hedge word" like *technically, strictly speaking,* and *in some* (or *a*) *sense.*

Example #1: Hedge Words

When we say that a tomato, "strictly speaking," is a fruit, we're showing that we're aware that different purposes entail different ways of classifying things—in this case, "scientific" versus "everyday." Here we and our audience are on common ground because we all know what the different classification systems are, even though most of us would be hard-put to explain exactly how a tomato is a fruit.

Example #2: Hedge Words

Strictly speaking, they weren't fired.

Technically, he didn't break the rules.

Their opinion is, in a sense, irrelevant.

Here we're hedging our labels by implying that there's another, equally legitimate classification—which we either spell out or leave to the audience's imagination.

In the first example, the writer could be saying that they weren't "fired" because nobody terminated their employment abruptly and without warning. It's just that their contracts weren't renewed or their positions were eliminated. But these events could still be <u>classified</u> as "firing," because the core, must-have segment of the word's meaning—that employment is terminated unilaterally, by the employer—is still there. <u>Technically</u>, though, they weren't fired.

Basically and essentially are two other popular hedge-words. Their meaning is "this is all the information that I am able (or willing) to present at the moment; anything I may have left out doesn't really matter."

Advice on Using Hedge Words

Since all hedge words imply a writer's decision about how a name is to be attached to a given piece of reality, be sure that your audience will accept your decisions. If they're not on the same wavelength, you have to be prepared to defend your hedgings (as with the "firing" example above).

Anticipating Objections to a Word Choice: "Pushing"

"Push-words," as the name implies, urge the audience to accept the writer's word-to-thing connections.

Push-Words: Category 1

true; truly; truth

fact(ual); in (point of) fact

real(ly); actual(ly)

These put the writer's stamp of approval on his/her own labelings of reality. That's really true (see? I just pushed you to accept my last statement). And the more you use them, the harder you're pushing.

Push-Words: Category 2

clear(ly)

evident(ly)

obvious(ly)

These push-words reinforce the writer's observations or conclusions. They say, "This is clear to me—and therefore to any other intelligent, right-thinking person." Obviously (get it?), they're great favorites of any writer or speaker whose conclusions aren't backed by hard evidence or solid reasoning processes.

Push-Words: Category 3

practically

virtually

The message of these two is "If there's any way in which the word I used seems not to apply to this reality, it's irrelevant; it doesn't matter." Observe a few cases of *virtually* or *practically* in action and you'll see how neatly writers use them to slide past situations in which someone else might call them on their word choice.

Negative Push-Words; Disagreeing with a Label

There's also a small group of negative push-words—*so-called* and *supposed(ly)*, as well as their upscale cousin *putative(ly)*. These are signs that the speaker disagrees with a label.

Here's how they work. The shorthand way to refer to a name–thing connection is to use *am/are/is/was/were*. So when we say, "This is an outrage," we're saying, in effect, "The conventional name for this event—and countless others like it— is *outrage*." But *so-called* or *supposed* before a word or phrase delivers a very powerful negative message: "This is not really [note the push-word] an outrage. I (the speaker/writer) disagree with and reject the word, because it doesn't name the thing accurately or appropriately."

WORD-CHOICE FUNCTION #2: JUDGING

Using Words to Express Our Feelings

The second function of word choice is to express your judgments and conclusions about the reality you're labeling.

Since everyday (as opposed to scientific) language allows us to use different words for the same thing, we have many opportunities to use a label that incorporates our feelings—and many reasons to do so.

Consider these examples of different names for the same thing.

> The Environmental Protection Agency substitutes fuzzy phrases for ominous terms: Talk of "a degree of hazard" becomes talk of "a degree of risk." Some EPA officials suggest calling enforcement personnel "compliance assistance officers." (*Wall Street Journal*)

> The White House "crisis management team" was replaced by the "special-situation group," which is made up of the same officials but renamed to avoid alarming the public each time it meets. (*U.S. News & World Report*)

> The Armed Forces, fearing a semblance of sexism, dropped the term "bachelor housing" in favor of "unaccompanied-personnel housing." (*Wall Street Journal*)

"What we need in Washington," said a wit named Bert Murray, "is a Department of Euphemisms—to help us understand what it is that the politicians are trying not to tell us."

Of course, Murray was kidding, precisely because the purpose of euphemisms—or "softeners," as I call them—is to label, with nice-sounding words, things that are not so nice.

Words have a way of getting associated with the things they stand for, and the euphemism helps to blur or even break the connection.

How Softeners Work

If you keep in mind that people can't tell it like it is—they can only agree (or disagree) about what to call it—you're well on the way toward understanding how softeners work. For a euphemism to be successful (that is, accepted by your audience), the audience must agree with you on two points:

1. the item or experience in question deserves to be labeled by a softener, and
2. this particular softener is the appropriate one.

The most consistently successful (that is, readily accepted) softeners are the ones that express **delicacy, tact, and propriety.** In this category are phrases like "pass away," "go to the men's/ladies' room," "make love," and all the many terms having to do with death, bodily processes, sex, physical or mental disability,[1] and other experiences that frighten and fascinate us. We're all comfortable with these softeners—that is, there's widespread agreement on point 1 above—and if someone deliberately avoids them, he/she does so in order to shock and disturb.

All other softeners enjoy varying degrees of success, generally because of disagreement about point 1. Many softeners, for example, may reflect a particular social or political point of view, as with *disadvantaged youth* (instead of *juvenile delinquent*), *substance abuser* (instead of *drug addict*), *inner city* (instead of *slum* or *ghetto*). But people who don't accept the underlying point of view (again, see point 1) will reject the word choice, arguing that, "He's not disadvantaged. He's a juvenile delinquent."

I can't tell you whether your softeners—or <u>any</u> softeners—will be successful. It all depends on the audience and context. The more radical the clash between the value systems of the writer/speaker and the audience in question, the more the audience is likely to reject the euphemism. The more similar the value systems, the likelier it is that the euphemism will be successful.

Where We Find Softeners

All euphemisms do the same thing: by renaming, they seek to redirect the audience's attitudes about the thing that they name. In addition to delicacy/propriety, here are some of the situations in which they're likely to be found (and in which you might want to consider using them).

- **Job and function titles:** *urban transportation specialist* (cab driver), *spirits merchant* (bartender), *environmental technician* (janitor), *advocate* (lobbyist, hustler, promoter)
- **Evaluations:** *visionary* (can't handle paperwork), *listens well* (has no ideas of his own), *consults with faculty* (indecisive)[2]
- **Government and business policymaking:** Here we find a wide variety—and a huge number—of softeners intended to mask realities that audiences might find disturbing.

  Businesses that cut staff may say they're "downsizing," "rightsizing," or "reengineering." And the government will claim to be "making investments" with our "contributions"; those who don't agree with the underlying philosophy would insist that the government is "redistributing" our "taxes" (and while leaders may say they're "asking" everyone to "contribute," has anyone ever told the IRS, "No, thanks—I'd rather not 'contribute' this year"?).
- **Unpleasant, undesirable, or downright disastrous events:** *negative patient outcome* (death), *rapid oxidation* (fire in a nuclear reactor)

The most consistently <u>un</u>successful euphemisms are in the last two categories. These euphemisms are the ones used to conceal odious policies: like *final solution, inoperative statements* (lies), *destabilizing* (overthrowing) *a government,* and *elimination with extreme prejudice* (murdering).

These softeners are unsuccessful because of vehement disagreement over point 1—the advisability of <u>using</u> a softener in the first place. If anyone is misled, it's usually only the labelers themselves. It's a sad fact, but language can help such people to evade moral accountability, if only in their own eyes.

Softeners: To Use or Not to Use?

Euphemisms enable us to talk comfortably about things we'd rather not—but nevertheless have to—talk about. On the other hand, they're often controversial and unsuccessful. At their worst, they disconnect language from reality, hinder communication, and breed contempt and mistrust.

In view of all this, should you avoid them? Should you (except where delicacy and propriety are called for) use the most direct word?

As an effective speaker, you seek to evoke a particular response in your audience. And the situations you encounter in everyday business and professional activities may actually call for you to choose your words so that they soften the impact of what you have to say, reduce the audience's sense of threat, or minimize its reaction.

The problem is that people are so used to softeners that this strategy is usually expected, so it only half-works; if your listeners know what's happening, they may just become <u>more</u> cynical, <u>more</u> suspicious of your motives. When I see *surcharge* on my phone bill, for example, it's easier to swallow than *additional amount that you'll have to pay*—but I still know I'll have to pay more.

The only way I can think of to use softeners effectively is to know your listeners. If the softener you're going to use implies something far different from the term they'd use, get out your dictionary and try something else. (On the other hand, if it's confrontation you seek, by all means use the most direct, uncompromising word you like—but be prepared to defend your choice.)

Word-Choice Function #2: Judgments (Continued): Using Language to Evaluate

The other piece of the "judgment" function of word choice involves descriptive words that evaluate. In each case, using a word appropriately means comparing your own evaluation to some standard—if there is one. The word *big*, for instance, can convey at least three different ideas of absolute size:

big bug (over an inch long?)

big dog (over 50 pounds?)

big elephant (more than 10 feet high?)

My question marks indicate some room for disagreement (to some people, any insect over one-quarter inch long is "big"). But at least we have a rough idea of the normal size of what we're describing.

Problem with Evaluators: No Agreed-Upon Point of Reference

But in all too many cases, there is no standard that everyone agrees on. A corporation announces a "revolutionary" new product, a "historic" labor settlement, or a "precedent-setting" joint venture, and the skeptic can justifiably ask,

"Compared to what?" After all, almost nothing is different in every way from everything that has gone before. Still, these evaluators do have some implied quality—novelty or distinctiveness—that the audience can assess against its experience. It's merely a question of how new—new enough to justify the use of *revolutionary*?

The same reasoning applies to *significant(ly), appreciable/ly, remarkable/ly, meaningful(ly), noteworthy, considerable/ly, relative(ly)*, or any other word that evaluates extent or importance. If you use these (e.g., "Our profits have increased *significantly"*), make sure that either your text or your context gives the reader a good reason to agree with you, or else the reaction is likely to be "'Significantly'?? That's not 'significant' to me!"

Your challenge is to make sure your evaluator accurately expresses your assessment—but is not too strong for your listeners. If you think they might consider your evaluator to be inappropriate, you'll need to supply information that will bring them around to your point of view.

Emotionally Loaded Evaluators

These words embody entire value systems: *(un)ethical, (im)moral, obscene, (in)sane, brave, foolish, liberal, bourgeois, sinful, cowardly,* and so on. Discovering the real-world meanings of these words takes anywhere from a few hours to a lifetime of study.

For our purposes, though, the instructions are simple: again, know your audience. Use emotionally loaded evaluators only if

1. you can establish a definition that your audience will agree with (if only provisionally or for the sake of discussion), or
2. you know that your audience already agrees with you.

WORD-CHOICE FUNCTION #3: DISTANCING

Selecting Words That Signal Your Relationship to Your Audience

Here we connect word choice to the distance (in the sense of "social space") between you and your audience. Let's begin with the **public/private** and **status** decisions. Ask yourself,

■ "Am I speaking to friends—or to social/organizational equals?" or,

■ "Am I making a public statement that will be heard by who-knows-how-many strangers—or by people who out-rank me socially or organizationally?"

Your choice of words can be determined by your answers to these questions. Or look at it the other way around: your choice of words can <u>signal</u> your answers to these questions— because it's very likely that your audience will hear your word choices in the way you intend them to be heard.

How to Use Word Choice as an Indicator of "Public/Private" and "Status"

Our language is rich in pairs of words that can label the same reality but are appropriate for different situations: pay/compensation, go/proceed, start/initiate, and so on. Sometimes one or the other will have a shade of meaning that better expresses what you want to say. But, other things being equal, *the more often you choose the longer, less "everyday"-sounding word, the more distance you're putting between yourself and your audience.*

If you're not sure about the message you're sending, check your dictionary. Labels such as "Informal" and "Colloquial," along with the dictionary's guide to what they mean (usually in the introduction to the dictionary), should point you in the right direction.

Word Choice and Style

The "personal" forms go quite naturally with the shorter, more-conversational-sounding words, while the "impersonal" forms go quite naturally with the less-familiar-sounding words. So make sure your grammatical and vocabulary choices send the same message.

Selecting Words That Signal In-Group Membership

In an ordinary office interaction, you might ask someone to "sign off on" something. By choosing the phrase *sign off on,* you've done two things:

1. you've asked for his/her written approval (that's just labeling), and
2. you've alluded indirectly to your common social bond as members of "white-collar business culture" by using the appropriate in-group term for "grant written approval."

Here correctness is determined by context. Business diction is correct for business audiences but jarringly inappropriate for people outside the business community. You ask corporate colleagues for their "input," academic colleagues for their "suggestions."

The same goes for every other form of slang and specialized vocabulary: word choice expresses powerful assumptions about your audience and your relationship to it. Effective writers choose words that echo and reinforce these relationships; they avoid words that violate them.

Learn the Lingo

A *Wall Street Journal* cartoon shows an executive telling one of his subordinates, "You'll never get anywhere around here, Fassler, until you start using *impact* as a verb." It's funny because nobody ever comes right out and tells you how you're supposed to talk if you're going to be "one of us"—but you pay attention and figure it out as fast as you can. If you're going to communicate within an organization, industry, trade association, government agency, or whatever, you want to find out what expressions are loved and loathed by those whom you have to answer to, and respond accordingly.

Buzzwords

Another *Wall Street Journal* cartoon: Irked manager tells underling, "Crampton, would you rewrite this memo using simple, straightforward buzzwords?"

Clearly, buzzwords are central to business and professional communication. But are they good or bad? That depends on which ones you use, and when.

A word or phrase is called a buzzword if it fulfills either—and sometimes both—of the following two criteria.

Buzzword Criterion #1: From the viewpoint of an out-group, the word is strongly associated with a particular in-group and is therefore offensive to those who dislike that group.

This is certainly the case with the use of *impact* as an action-word (as in "the work stoppage will adversely impact our profits"). Those who don't like businesspeople tend not to like this use of *impact.*

Another reason why this usage is so popular, I suspect, is that it offers an easy escape for people who can't keep straight the difference between *affect* ("to have an influence on") and *effect* (two meanings: "to bring about" and "an influence or result"). Now you do know the difference, so use *impact* carefully, and only in ways that serve your purposes.

Buzzword Criterion #2: From the viewpoint of an in-group, the word refers to something that is either newly discovered or newly important.

Quality is the buzzword in manufacturing circles nowadays.

Everybody's talking about the information super-highway; it's become our national buzzword.

The meaning of the Criterion 2 buzzwords is typically vague: just because they are so new, there's no consensus about what reality they label. This phenomenon is responsible for the term itself—when they encounter a buzzword, audiences hear only a buzz.

A buzzword can either undermine your effectiveness as a communicator (you violate Criterion #1 and use it inappropriately, with an out-group) or reinforce it (you fulfill Criterion #2 and use it appropriately, with an in-group). So you must either avoid buzzwords or use them effectively, as the situation requires.

In all cases, be sensitive to the fact that the meaning of your buzzword can be squishy. If you intend (and you think your audience will hear) it as a feel-good word that labels something that you all approve of, fine; but if you're using it as a softener (e.g., *restructuring* instead of *layoffs*), follow my advice on softeners.

THE RIGHT WORD: SUMMARY, WHAT IT MEANS TO "USE A WORD CORRECTLY"

At this point, you should have a pretty good grasp of how to make correct word choices. The "right" word (or phrase) is the one that does all of the following:

- It symbolizes reality in a way that your audience will agree with.

■ It embodies your feelings and conclusions about that reality, in a way that your audience can accept.

■ It sends accurate information about (1) the relationship between you and your audience (personal/impersonal), or (2) the social context (public/private) in which the communication takes place, or (3) the group membership(s) of writer/speaker and audience.

If you use words that do all of the above, your audience won't dispute your word choice. If you think some readers/listeners might, you can defend your decision, if only briefly, in your text. To put it another way, "misusing" words is usually an inappropriate—and unexplained—choice in one of the above three areas.

But we're not quite done. There are three other pitfalls (or "challenges," if you will) on your path to consistently correct word choices.

WORD-CHOICE CHALLENGE #1: LANGUAGE VARIABILITY AND CHANGE

Liberals and Conservatives

Our language is constantly in transition, and new words—as well as new meanings for old words—are constantly being added to its resources. The problem for people who want to speak and write correctly is that editors, English teachers, columnists, and other language authorities typically see these additions and variations not as change in progress—but as mistakes.

So there's constant tension between language "liberals," who recognize this growth and change for what it is and are thus quick to accept new usages (especially those that serve a clear purpose), and "conservatives," who grudgingly admit that language does change, but still cling to the view that departures from accepted usage are wrong until they become "accepted" (by the very same authorities who are saying they're wrong!)

Given all this inconsistency and circularity, how are real-world writers, like you and me, supposed to make the right choices?

Language in Transition: How to Identify Correct Word Usages

Step 1: Begin by identifying the words that might be a problem for you. The good news is that they're very few in number, considering the enormous vocabulary of our language. To learn what they are, look in any English handbook under "Exact Words," "Diction," or "Misused Words."

Step 2: Now match your own usage against that list. You may already be using many of the "correct" versions. But remember, your source represents only the opinion of one authority at one point in time. You're not going to find ultimate truth in a handbook.

Step 3: Compare your own "incorrect" usages with (1) a very recent dictionary, and (2) the speech patterns of those around you, especially those who have "edit power" over you (i.e., the power to determine the final form of your message—and it may be you). You will thus find out whether a particular transitional usage is "provisionally acceptable" or "unacceptable."

"**Provisionally acceptable**" usages are those that have become so well established that only the most conservative textbooks and authorities are still riled up about them.

Examples of provisionally correct usages:

1. The use of *infer* to mean "hint" or "imply." Traditionally, *imply* meant "hint," and *infer* meant "conclude," as in

"He put on his coat, so I inferred that he was leaving."
But *infer* has been used to mean "imply" so often and for
so long that many dictionaries report that they can
indeed mean the same thing.

2. *Hopefully* as an expression of hope on the part of the
speaker/writer, as in "Hopefully, the weather will clear up"
or "We will hopefully complete the report by tomorrow."
Again, this is a usage you'll find in any recent dictionary,
though conservatives continue to insist on *I hope* or *It is
to be hoped.*

If you're using a word your handbook considers incorrect
but that a recent dictionary says is OK, then go ahead and use
it, especially in the personal style and especially if you have
edit power. But if it's going to be a problem for someone else
who's more conservative and who has edit power, go with the
more conservative usage.

An "**unacceptable**" usage is one that both your handbook and your dictionary agree has not yet become appropriate for general use. The dictionary either will not mention it
at all or will flag it with a label like "Nonstandard." That's
your cue to avoid it altogether. An example (as of 1997) is
irregardless, a blend of *regardless* and *irrespective*. Use either one
("*Regardless* of/ *Irrespective* of my own beliefs, I'll be happy to
listen to you"), but not *irregardless*.

How to Be Correct All the Time

Don't worry about memorizing the "correct" choices in your
handbook all at once, because you have many alternative
routes available. Just avoid the word you know to be trouble-
some, and find some other way to say the same thing. Lots of
practice and reading will lodge the *imply/infer* distinction
firmly in your mind. Until that happens, use *hint* and *conclude* (or *guess*).

WORD-CHOICE CHALLENGE #2:
GENDER AND OTHER SENSITIVITIES

About 70 years ago, a linguist named Benjamin Whorf theo-rized that the grammar and vocabulary of a language could influence the way the speakers of that language view the world. Later—about 30 years ago—a group of feminists applied Whorf's theory (which has never been conclusively proven) to modern English as an argument for change in the way we use the language.

Their reasoning goes like this: If we go on using words like *mankind* and *mailman*, and sentences like "A doctor might use the new drug on *his* patient," then we will in effect be writing women off—ignoring the fact that they are more than half of our species, dismissing the possibility that they can be doctors, and so on.

I can't tell you whether this argument is true or not. But what's important for our purposes is the fact that most liter-ate people now <u>regard</u> it as true. So if you fail to use language that is gender-neutral, you risk offending your audience. But stick to the following principles, and you'll be all right.

Gender-Neutral Communication, Principle #1: When writing about people generally, avoid *man* and all words that contain it and imply "male"—replace with gender-neutral words.

Thus, instead of *mankind*, use *people* or *humanity* (some hard-liners won't even let you get by with that because it has *man* in it), or *men and women*; instead of *businessman*, use (*business*) *executive*, *manager* (or *account executive*, or whatever job title applies); instead of *Congressman*, use *Representative, Senator, Congressperson, Legislator,* or *Congressional Representative.*

Gender-Neutral Communication, Principle #2: Avoid using *he/his/him* to point back to an indefinite word or phrase.

The neatest solution is to make the indefinite word/phrase into a plural (that is, add -*(e)s f*or a "more than one" meaning); then you can use *they/their/them*: "Doctors might use the new drug on *their* patients."

To point back to an indefinite *everybody/somebody/anybody*, use *him or her, him/her, his or her, his/her* (with the slash-mark), or *a(n)* (but NOT *they/their/them*; this alternative is currently OK only in very informal personal style or in spoken language).

Examples of gender-marked and gender-neutral language:

Gender-marked: Everybody received *his* paycheck.

Neutral: Everybody received *his or her* [or *a*] paycheck.

If the *his or her* sounds too awkward, see if you can't revise and get rid of the wild-card word entirely:

Gender-marked: Does anybody want this office assigned to *him*?

Neutral (awkward): Does anybody want this office assigned to *him or her*?

Neutral (better): This office will be assigned to someone. Does anyone want it?

Gender-Neutral Communication, Principle #3: Avoid using *she/her* to refer to words that denote traditionally female occupations. Again, the double

pronoun may be intolerably awkward, and you may have to rewrite:

Gender-marked: Give this to one of the secretaries; *she'll* type it.

Neutral (awkward): Give this to one of the secretaries. *He or she* will type it.

Neutral (better): If you want this typed, give it to one of the secretaries.

Gender Sensitivity: Overcompensating

Some speakers and writers like to flaunt their gender sensitivity by using *she* and *her* to refer to an indefinite word earlier in the sentence, even though there's no reason to believe that the person in question is female (e.g., "A doctor might use the new drug on *her* patients"). If you really want to impress the hard-line gender warriors in your audience, go ahead. But my guess is that everyone else will be either confused ("'Her'?? Who's he talking about?") or irritated by this self-conscious proclamation of gender sensitivity and political correctness.

Word Choice and Ethnic Sensitivity

The political correctness movement of the 1990s has also raised a new sensitivity about labels for groups who consider themselves oppressed and therefore demand the right to decide what they should be called, in some cases discarding labels devised by others.

Thus, blacks, having fought to rid themselves of such unacceptable labels as "colored people" and "Negroes," are

now to be known as "African Americans" (at least in the first
mention in a text; thereafter, *black* is OK); they also join His-
panics and Asians as "people of color." Many politically liberal media supported the trend; the *Portland Oregonian*, out of
respect for Native Americans, referred to the Washington Red-
skins as "Washington's football team."

Be alert to ethnic sensitivities and to changing linguistic
fads. If you like, buy a guidebook or electronic editor to help
you identify specific words to use and avoid.[3] But if you regu-
larly read newspapers and watch TV news, you'll have plenty
of exposure to what's considered ethnically sensitive usage.

WORD-CHOICE CHALLENGE #3:
BALANCING ORIGINALITY AND FAMILIARITY

Refuse to use clichés, we're told.
Make your writing fresh and bold.
So lest my prose be weak and trite,
I just won't read what others write!

Nom DePlume

As you look over your word choices, you want to be sure
you've achieved a balance between originality and familiarity.

This advice might seem to contradict what we learned in
our English classes about not using clichés. But Mr. DePlume
has a valid point: how are you supposed to avoid clichés
when communication consists in large measure of words and
phrases that audiences will recognize?

The answer may surprise you, but it's the one that works
for me: you don't have to avoid them. You need only understand them so that you can make the right choices about
their use.

Understanding Clichés—The Case for Familiarity

To begin with, the question "What is a cliché?" has no simple answer. Clichés acquire their status over a period of time, as a group of words is repeatedly used together, by one writer after another. There's no Cliché Control Board that can deliver expert and binding opinions ("As of midnight, December 31, 1998, the following expressions are considered clichés . . . ").

Instead, triteness is a subjective reaction. It's an informal consensus among literate people—the result of repeated encounters, by an ever-widening range of individuals, with a particular sequence of words. Like correctness, originality is a moving target.

Second, originality is a literary value; that's why English teachers are so enamored of it. But 100-percent-original word- and phrase-choices are not only impractical in every-day business and professional communication; they're not even necessary.

The fact is that familiarity isn't all bad. Here are some pretty familiar phrases that I found in the transcript of a speech by the CEO of a major financial institution:

Monday-morning quarterbacks

an endangered species

predict with confidence

raised it to an art form

take a dim view

an article of faith

paved the way

rush in to fill the void

made a mockery of

the argument rages

a new situation under the sun

a dim understanding

Hackneyed writing? I know what the obvious answer is, but let's examine the other side of the you-know-what. That speech was over twenty-five hundred words long. It contained a number of fairly subtle points, and it covered some difficult technological issues. What kept the audience's mind engaged through all of this? Variety, that's what—the alternation between the predictable and the unpredictable.

Another reason why familiarity isn't all bad has to do with the audience. Using the word or phrase that's appropriate to speaker, audience, and subject is one of the components of good style. As I pointed out earlier in this chapter (remember the example of *sign off*), it's a way of reinforcing the bond between writer/speaker and audience.

Familiarity can be very powerful. Commonly and strongly held beliefs—corporate and institutional mission statements, for instance—are typically repeated in the same words every time. Prayers, to take an extreme case, are virtually unchangeable.

Consider the memo that Arch McGill distributed, back in the mid-1980s, to everyone in AIS/American Bell on the first day of the new organization's existence. It was published as a two-page spread in a number of major newspapers, and it articulated almost every one of the basic tenets of American business, in exactly the correct terms: *dynamic marketplace, profound contribution to society, meet customer needs, search for excellence, the talent/skills/commitment, quality service, the competitive arena,* and others.

Advice: Originality/Familiarity of Word Choice

Think beyond simplistic values like "trite" and "fresh," and strive for effectiveness by balancing words and expressions that are familiar to the audience with those that are not.

In particular, if your text contains many new concepts and propositions, it's OK to introduce, link, explain, and discuss them with an occasional tried and true (there's one!) expression. But if your subject matter is itself familiar, your discussion might be more effective if you spent a little time with your dictionary (or the electronic thesaurus in your word processor) in search of more imaginative word choices that could help your audience to view the subject in a new way.

Second, know your audience; make strategic use of the words and phrases that emphasize what you have in common with them.

Third, know your editor (if there is someone who has edit power over your speech text); if he/she thinks something is trite (or a buzzword, in the negative sense), then you should avoid it.

In particular, if your editor (or the person for whom you are ghostwriting) has a humanities background, you should expect more antagonism toward business diction (e.g., *prioritize, time-frame, finalize*) than if he/she is a pure-business type (trained in finance, engineering, chemistry, and so on).

Finally, if you're speaking about—or even briefly referring to—an organization's history, values, culture, or mission, be sure to use the traditional, accepted words and phrases (consult existing documents for guidelines and examples).

NOTES

1. As of this writing (1997), American society is in the grip of a "political correctness" mania that has spawned a host of new softeners in this category. You'll want to be sensitive to the expectations of your audience. The trend has apparently peaked, as evidenced by the fact that it is now the subject of ridicule (e.g., a cartoon that assigns politically correct names to the Seven Dwarfs—Dopey becomes "Differently Intellectually Abled"; Grumpy, "Poor Anger Management Skills").

2. Examples and translations are from a University of Southern California faculty memo written to help members of a search commit-

tee understand what was really meant in candidates' letters of reference (published in the July 1989 issue of *Harper's*).

3. But these are no substitute for the human eye and brain. An editing program that purports to make a text gender- and ethnicity-sensitive went overboard and changed the word *black* once too often, thus causing an article to report that "the company's finances were once again in the African American."

10 Delivering the Message

SELECTING YOUR SUPPORT STRATEGY

As you work on your speech, start thinking about the kind of support you'll need when you deliver it.

The key point about speech support is that every speech comes from somewhere, whether that source is visible or invisible. Even when you're called upon to give an impromptu, completely unrehearsed toast, you draw on your background knowledge of the occasion, the toastee(s), and the specific form and length of a toast.

This invisible support can be quite extensive. I'm impressed—but never fooled—by polished political or business speakers who say they "wing it" without script or notes. I'm aware that they've thought and talked about their subject so much that mental notes—even mental audio cassettes—are cued up and ready to go; all the speaker has to do is turn to page 1 or hit PLAY.

If you don't know your subject that well, you'll need visible support. But how much? There's a wide range of possibilities, from an index card with the sparest of memory-joggers/thought-starters, to outlines thick and thin, to a full script.[1] You can even do hybrids: a script with ad lib sections, a set of notes with a scripted (or memorized) opening and close.

Your choice depends on several factors:

▪ **Your familiarity with the subject.** As with the experi-
enced business or political speaker, if your subject and
message are already well understood and well rehearsed,
you may need only the thinnest support. However, since
most of my speeches are "one-offs," I generally go with a
script, because my material is familiar—but not so well rehearsed that I've internalized it.

▪ **Your tendency to get stage fright.** Stage fright isn't all
bad. As rock guitarist John Cipollina says, it's "nature's
way of preventing us from being stupid all the time."[2] But
if it's a problem for you, simply increase the level of support—to a full script if necessary—to lower the demands
on your nervous system.

▪ **Your verbal fluency.** Listen to a conversation, and you'll
hear how fluently most people, including yourself, can
speak without preparation. But even if you know your
material cold, ask yourself: "How well can I compose
smooth, grammatical, full, meaningful sentences, one
after another, in logical sequence, under pressure, with a
minimum of garble and false starts, in a nonconversation-
al mode?" Of course, with practice, you can learn to do
this. But if the answer right now is, "Not too well," consider raising the level of your support.

▪ **Time limitations.** In a time-constrained situation, if your
level of support is higher, you'll be less likely to digress
and ramble—and better able to keep on track and use
your available time efficiently.

▪ **Delicacy of your subject.** If you need to express your
thoughts precisely and avoid being misunderstood, consider scripting at least part of your speech.

▪ **Technicality of your subject.** If you need to explain difficult concepts precisely or build intricate ideational structures, use higher levels of support—especially if time is
limited.

▪ **Need for cogency and persuasiveness.** "Sharing a few
thoughts off the cuff" is different from a clutch speech
that has to accomplish something specific. The repeated
revision involved in preparing a script will help you devel-

op the most effective way to get your message across; you're not likely to hit it on the first, spontaneous try.

■ **Need for quotability and permanence.** If you want or expect your speech to be quoted to—or read in full by—people beyond the immediate audience, consider using a script and distributing it afterward (alternate procedure: speak into a tape recorder, then transcribe what you said).

SPEECHMAKING AS ACTING

Remember, as you choose and design your support, that the desired end-result is always the same: you want the fluency, conciseness, and coherence of a script, plus the appearance of the spontaneity of an impromptu talk (I say "appearance" because, as I noted above, even speakers who seem to be great at winging it . . . rarely are). That's what an acting performance is—and you are, in a sense, an actor.

The character you're playing is yourself. You want to be the most persuasive, effective YOU that you can be. Unlike the performances of Paul Newman or Meryl Streep, who create totally different characters in each picture, your acting is more like that of Kevin Costner, Robert Redford, Ted Danson, or Tom Selleck, who pretty much play themselves, but with the appropriate attitude and emotion. Along with these narrow-range actors, there are two other kinds of performers who can help you.

KEY TO EFFECTIVE DELIVERY: MODELING

Newscasters and news commentators are excellent models. The low level of the intensity of their material, plus the limited range of emotion with which they deliver it (no shouting or arm waving, no matter how exciting the story is), are pretty close to the presentational "you" that will be appropriate for most situations.

So observe their steady eye contact, confident demeanor, and precise diction. Listen to the way they vary their pacing—how they dwell on the more important, less familiar words and phrases and move briskly through the rest. Notice especially the way they use nuances of voice and facial gesture to impart emotion to—and communicate their own attitudes toward—their material. Watch the newscaster's face as he/she reads the opening story about a plane crash, and compare that with the expression he/she uses for the final, "fluff" story.

Standup comedians and talk and game show hosts are also good models. If newscasters can show you how to deliver a script, these other performers can show you how to speak unscripted in an audience-engaging way.

Of course, I'm not advising you to ape their bizarre mannerisms. Rather, the point is to notice how they interact with the audience. Maybe you can even use some of their interactive techniques yourself (e.g., "How many of you have heard of . . . ? Let me see a show of hands.").

Note also the informality of their language—not the profanity, of course, but the easy conversational style that will, unless your subject is really serious, be far more appropriate for most of your speech situations than the ponderous formal prose we see in most written documents (and in speeches at self-important forums like the United Nations).

HOW TO DELIVER A SCRIPT WITH IMPACT

Speaking from a script doesn't have to be dull. A few basic strategies will enable you to leverage the inherent advantages of a script—conciseness, precision, preservability, clarity of organization, and effectiveness of opening and closing—into a forceful and memorable presentation.

Essentially you'll do what actors do when they read lines: identify your role and motivation, then use voice qualities, pauses, and eye contact to convey the way you feel about your audience and your message.

First, go through your script and find the places where one or both of the following is especially clear:

■ The role you're playing (colleague, motivator/coach, teacher, leader, bearer of good/bad news, etc.)
■ Your attitude/perspective on what you're saying.

Then, at each of these points, mark your script as follows:

■ Use marginal notes to give yourself "stage directions," for example:

> Make them feel great.
> UPBEAT
> Get their attention.
> LEADERLY
> GRATEFUL
> WARM, FRIENDLY
> HOPEFUL
> SKEPTICAL
> CURIOUS, PUZZLED
> Reassure them.
> TENSION, PROBLEM, CHALLENGE
> This is the solution!

■ In the text itself, use indicators of pitch, pause, and intensity to supplement and execute the stage directions.
  • Highlight words and phrases that are key to the attitudes you wish to convey; the highlighting will focus your attention on these and ensure that they're delivered with the appropriate emphasis and intensity.
  • Use accent marks for emphasis.
  • Draw faces (☺) as emotional cues.
  • Use wavy lines to give yourself the appropriate pitch and intonation cues, for example:

> So yes, we have made a lot of progress. But there's still much more to do.

These "intonation contours" will also remind you to widen your pitch range, thus avoiding monotony.

- Insert slashes to indicate pauses (/ for short pause, // for medium, /// for long). Pauses should go . . .

  ✔ in your "laundry lists," after each point, reason, strategy, etc.;

  ✔ between sections of your talk (the more important the boundary, the longer the pause);

  ✔ after conclusions and "clinchers," where the pause gives the audience a moment to ponder;

  ✔ before numbers, complex ideas, striking figures of speech, or anything else that, if you were speaking off the cuff, you'd need a moment to recall or make up.

■ In the margins, write "EC" at the points where you want to be sure you're making eye contact with your audience. HINT: There should be lots of eye contact whenever you're speaking in the "you" mode. Also, it's OK to look down at your script for your next point, reason, example, objective, etc. The audience assumes that you'll have notes or some other kind of support.

Now you have a script plus a set of instructions for delivering it. If you practice executing your own stage directions, you will effectively communicate not only your words and ideas, but also your attitudes about them, your feelings behind them, and the drama within them.

REHEARSAL AND EVALUATION

I'm going to say it only once: practice. Over and over. Until you can practically say it in your sleep. And use as many feedback techniques as you can—audio tape, video tape, mirror, and, yes, a loved one who is willing to sit through your presentation and be brutally frank.

Repeated practice will (1) fine-tune your message (practice is simply the final stage in the composing process); (2) help ingrain your message in your mind, thus preventing faltering and stage fright; (3) help you identify words that are difficult for you to pronounce or that sound like other words; (4) tell you how long your speech is, so that you can make it fit your time limit; and, of course, (5) improve your command of the fundamentals.

Here's a checklist:

Head

✓ DO: nod, shake to affirm and reinforce speech content.

✗ DON'T: nod excessively (that's approval-seeking; not powerful).

✗ DON'T: twitch, make nervous movements.

Eyes

✓ DO: fix on individuals.

✓ DO: use your eyes to "act out" your text (e.g., look up if thinking; look at audience when in "you" mode; look puzzled when pondering difficult question).

✗ DON'T: look down at your notes or script for long periods (if you wear glasses that reflect light, try to keep your head up because it's very hard for the audience to see your eyes).

✗ DON'T: sweep audience.

✗ DON'T: stare off into the distance for long periods.

✗ DON'T: let your eyes dart about, blink, or twitch excessively.

Smile

✓ DO: when content warrants it (e.g., when reciting pleasant amenities at beginning; when talking about positive realities).

✗ DON'T: smile nervously when content doesn't warrant (too approval-seeking).

Hands

✓ DO: use natural gestures that act out content, for example:

- TREND ("Profits rose steadily . . . ")
- NUMBERS ("We have four goals . . . ")
- GLOBAL ("The organization as a whole . . . ")
- DIFFERENCES/DISJUNCTIONS ("There's a sharp contrast between . . . "; use "cutting" or "cleaving" gestures)
- POINTING ("It's right here—in our organization")

✓ DO: rest hands naturally on lectern (and alternate that with something else—e.g., handling prop, pencil, pointer).

✓ DO: use gestures appropriate to space and audience (e.g., smaller, more confined gestures for a smaller audience and space).

✗ DON'T: lean on lectern.

✗ DON'T: grasp lectern rigidly.

✗ DON'T: use mini-gestures (e.g, twitching fingers while resting hands on lectern) or meaningless gestures.

✗ DON'T: keep hands stiff at sides (relaxed is OK).

✗ DON'T: clasp hands or arms in front.

✗ DON'T: engage in nervous mannerisms (playing with prop/pointer/chalk/marker; jingling change in pocket; repeatedly touching ear, nose, chin, face for self-reassurance).

Voice

✓ DO: keep pitch as low as comfortable (suggests authority).

✓ DO: vary tone and intensity to "act out" text.

✓ DO: keep energy up (suggests conviction, strength).

✗ DON'T: speak in monotone.

✗ DON'T: whisper, speak with low intensity (suggests lack of conviction).

Pacing

✓ As rapid as is comfortable (remember: speech flows at only 125 words per minute, but listening comprehension is 300+ wpm).

✓ IMPORTANT: Use "slow/fast" pacing; vary your pace with the importance of your content and the (un)familiarity of your words and ideas; move briskly through familiar material, but linger on the important or the unfamiliar.

✓ Make strategic use of pauses to separate sections of the speech (especially before the conclusion) or to let an important point sink in.

Pronunciation/Diction

✓ It's not easy to change deep-seated habits, but try to mitigate gross signals of regional/social dialects that are different from the speech patterns of your audience (e.g., dropping of -r, pronunciation of *both* with *f*, especially if these speech features are so prominent as to create a distraction or to make one word sound like another. The same applies to nonprestige pronunciations (insofar as you can spot them)—they diminish your image.

✓ Eliminate meaningless hesitation-forms and connectives—*uh, ah, er, so, then.*

Body

✓ Stay relaxed; face your audience head-on.

✓ It's OK to turn your body, especially with a large group, if you're not too mechanical about it.

✓ It's OK to lean toward the audience if the content is appropriate.

✓ Your posture should be erect but not rigid; no leaning (suggests lack of strength).

FINAL PREPARATIONS

Whatever your mode of support, print it out in as large a type font as you need. Allow for poor lighting.

When you print out your script, don't let any one sentence continue from one page to the next. Insert hard page breaks so that you never have to change pages in the middle of a sentence.

If you're speaking in an informal setting without a lectern, print your speech out on four-by-six-inch cards (even if it's a script). They're easier to handle and much less conspicuous than sheets of paper.

If you have a lectern, print your speech out on $8\frac{1}{2}$-by-11-inch heavyweight bond paper. It's easier to handle; the sheets won't stick together.

As you talk, slide the top page unobtrusively to the left (heavyweight paper makes it much easier to do this); don't flip pages. Consider using a Script-Master;[3] with this ingenious "speech box," you can almost completely conceal your support (and you can carry your speech in it, too).

Break a leg!

NOTES

1. Of course, if you're a Toastmaster or an aspiring professional speaker, you'll want to memorize your speech, or use the thinnest possible support. You can write a script in order to crystallize your ideas, sequence your material, and find the right words. Then, as you practice your delivery, you'll reduce your visible support to notes and ultimately to nothing at all.

2. Quoted in "Butterflies lurk everywhere among the glib and the dead," *Chicago Tribune*, Jan. 25, 1987.

3. Obtainable from SCRIPT-MASTER™ Division, Brewer-Cantelmo Co., Inc., 116 E. 27th St., New York, NY 10016.

Bringing It All Together: Practicing What I Preach

Let's look at an entire speech, from beginning to end, to see how I've applied the principles in this book. Its title is "Progress through Innovation—You Can't Have One without the Other." It was a keynote address, delivered on April 3, 1992, by Robert G. McVicker, Senior Vice President, Technology, Quality Assurance, and Scientific Relations, Kraft General Foods, at the 1992 Leaders of the Future Engineering Conference, held at Pennsylvania State University.

> Good evening . . . and let me say right off the bat that I'm delighted to be here with so many of you leaders of the future. And I can hardly think of a more appropriate topic for tomorrow's leaders to be thinking about . . . than progress and innovation . . . because, let's face it, to some degree, you're going to be responsible for the progress of the society in which you will be leaders.[1] And so I thought I might help you prepare for that role, by offering a few thoughts on just what innovation is . . . why we need it . . . how we get it . . . and how you can help bring it about.[2]
>
> First, let's get some idea of what innovation is.[3] Back in the late 19th and early 20th centuries, there was a great German chemist named Johann von Baeyer. He made many contributions to science, and in 1905, he was awarded a Nobel Prize.[4] One morning, Baeyer came into his laboratory and found that his assistants had built an ingenious mechanical stirring

device operated by water turbines. The professor was fascinated by the complex machine, and he summoned his wife from their apartment next door. For a while, Frau Baeyer watched the apparatus in silent admiration. And then she exclaimed, "What a lovely idea for making mayonnaise!"

There's a basic distinction to be made here: the good professor's students were the inventors—but his wife was the innovator. As Peter Drucker[5] says, "above all, innovation is not invention. It is a term of economics rather than of technology. The measure of innovation is the impact on the environment." Innovation, according to Drucker, "allows resources the capacity to create wealth."

But invention and innovation don't necessarily happen together. In fact, if you look at the history of science, you find that very often the application of a new idea has lagged the idea itself, by many years, sometimes centuries.

One reason may be that the supporting technologies don't yet exist to make the invention fully functional.[6] Five hundred years ago, Leonardo da Vinci envisioned a flying machine . . . an armor-plated tank, complete with firearms . . . a portable bridge . . . a cannon that worked like a modern machine gun . . . battleships . . . mechanically propelled armored cars . . . even an "ideal city"—but of course, he never built them.

And let's say you do create a one-of-a-kind model.[7] That doesn't automatically mean that you can turn it into a useful, functional, marketable device. It often takes someone else to do that, and perhaps with just one twist-of-the-wrist modification.[8] The transistor was invented in Bell Laboratories in 1947. Yet Sony sold the first transistor radio in America in 1956. In that same year Ampex, a U.S. company, introduced the first videotape recorder—but Sony improved its design and introduced its Betamax in 1975.

If innovation is to follow invention,[9] the social and economic conditions have to be right, too. There had

been many primitive calculating devices—going all the
way back to Leibniz—before William Burroughs
invented his adding machine in 1894. But by then, the
time was right. Business and industry were getting
pretty complicated, and Burroughs's invention was
quickly commercialized and saved people from the
endless toil of calculation, just as the inventor
intended.

But earlier in the 19th century, a genius named
Charles Babbage had conceived—and even partially
built—an extraordinary data processing device which
he called an "analytical engine." At the time, few if
any saw the implications of Babbage's work. It wasn't
until the Second World War, when military people
needed to rapidly calculate the trajectories of artillery
shells, that the first true computers appeared—and in
structure and function, they were remarkably similar
to the analytical engine of Charles Babbage.

So we have invention . . . and we have
innovation.[10] And it's innovation that's essential to
progress. In the words of Theodore Levitt, editor of the
Harvard Business Review,[11] "Just as energy is the basis of
life itself, and ideas the source of innovation, so is
innovation the vital spark of all man-made change,
improvement and progress."

Why is innovation so critical to the success of
countries, and even to the future of humanity?[12]
Because it's the raw material for the creation of wealth;
everything else is just reshuffling and redistribution of
what we already have. Just as a lever dramatically
increases the amount of force you can exert, so does
innovation raise productivity, spur economic growth
and increase wealth.[13] In a world where everything has
its price, technological innovation—though it's not
without its costs—is still the closest thing there is to an
economic free lunch.[14]

And I'm not just talking about recent innovations
like the automobile, the telephone, or the computer.
The ancient Greeks gave us the lever, wedge, pulley,
and gear. (In fact, sometime in the first century, Hero

of Alexandria even invented a coin-operated vending machine to dispense holy water!) In the Middle Ages came the horseshoe and stirrup, which revolutionized transportation and warfare . . . as well as the chimney, which facilitated home cooking and allowed us to get presents from Santa Claus. Islamic society gave us paper. And the Chinese invented matches, the umbrella, and the toothbrush.

My point is that many of what now seem to us to be the most mundane of contraptions . . . actually had a profound effect on human progress. The wealth, comforts, and living standards we enjoy today . . . are built upon thousands of years of innovations, many of which are now so common that it's hard to think that there was a time when they didn't exist.[15]

But every generation makes its contributions, just as you will make yours.[16] And that's why, now that you know a little about what innovation is, it's important to get some idea of how innovation takes place— in societies, in organizations, and in individuals.[17] I'll talk a little about the first two, but I'm going to devote most of my time to the third, because while your influence on organizations and on society are some years off, there are some things you can do right now, as individuals, that can help make you the innovators and, yes, the leaders of the future.[18]

The question of what drives innovation in a society is a tough one that nobody has a definitive answer to.[19] You need a supply of good ideas, plus an environment in which they can develop. So a society's level of education . . . its willingness to bear risk . . . the tolerance of its religion and its political structure . . . and its general openness to new ideas—probably all have something to do with it. Even factors as diverse as good nutrition and property rights may play a role. But when everything comes together, watch out![20] It's probably no coincidence that in ancient Greece and the Renaissance, there was extraordinary innovation not only in science, but in literature and art as well.

Of course, war is a great motivator, a shock to the system, a forcer of innovation for survival.

As I mentioned earlier, war helped bring about the first modern computers. A few decades earlier, it was the First World War that drove the Germans to find a new kind of marine propulsion system—an alternative to paddle wheels. They came up with screw-driven, thrust-bearing propellers. The concept had been known about for a hundred years (and the screw goes back to the ancient Greeks, remember?) . . . the lubricants and materials already existed—but engineers had never had such a powerful reason to bring them all together. And of course, the classic example is the Manhattan Project, which, in the interests of winning World War II, created the atomic bomb and changed the course of history.

The innovations that had the most powerful effect on living standards, including some of the ones I mentioned, are discussed in a very interesting book called *The Lever of Riches*, which was published last year. The author, Joel Mokyr, argues that there's no single set of conditions that guarantee technological innovation. And he reminds us that progress cannot be taken for granted, because there are such powerful forces that oppose it and enforce the status quo.[21]

Look at what happened in China. Before 1400, the Chinese were the most advanced civilization on earth. Before Columbus was even born, they were sending out huge "treasure ships," with crews of five hundred, all the way to the Persian Gulf and East Africa. One expedition brought back a giraffe, which was something of a culture shock to the folks back in Peking. The ships could have made it all the way to West Africa and Europe. And with all of their inventions and innovations, the Chinese may even have been within reach of the kind of industrial revolution that took place in Europe.

Then, suddenly, it was all over. And nobody knows exactly why.[22] All we know is that the government was in charge of invention and innovation . . . and at some point, it lost interest in technological progress. The bureaucrats, the custodians of the status quo, got the upper hand, they decided that the wealth of the Empire was to be spent on public-works projects that would improve the lot of the nation's farmers—and that was that.[23] Leadership in technology began to shift to Western civilization, where it remains to this day.

Well, so much for what innovation is . . . and the kind of social environment that's conducive to it. Now let's narrow our focus and zoom in on business organizations, especially the science- and technology-based companies in which many of you will spend at least part, maybe even all of your careers. How can they be organized for innovation?[24]

Let me begin my answer with a comparison. I'll ask you to think about the difference between basketball and football as a metaphor for differences in management . . . and by "management," I mean simply the most effective marshaling of human talent to get things done.[25] Traditionally, American businesses operated like football teams—but it's the basketball team that's the model for the management style of the '90s and beyond.

You see, in football, we find narrow specialization of function—centers, linebackers, tackles, even special teams. The individual players at some positions tend to be interchangeable parts. But basketball puts a premium on generalized skills: though some players excel at scoring, playmaking, and so on, everyone must pass, dribble, shoot, play defense, and rebound.

In football, the players pause and regroup after each play, and one player—or the coach—decides what the team will do next. But basketball is too dynamic to permit rigid separation of planning and execution, which is what the football huddle is all about. The team has a number of set plays, but it can't rely on them for every situation.

The point here is that to be the leading innovators in our world of rapidly advancing technology and global competition, we in U.S. industry have to learn to move quickly—to constantly improve our products and, most importantly, our manufacturing processes, within ever-shortening time frames.

And to do that, we have to be less like a football team—and more like a basketball team. We need to integrate specialist and generalist, managing and working, planning and doing. Specifically,[26] we need to move people from one job to another to give them breadth . . . we need to make sure people have as much autonomy as they can handle, and we need to act as quickly as possible on what seem to be good ideas—in other words, we need to avoid paralysis by analysis.

But that's not the only way to organize for innovation.[27] Another is to form cross-functional teams, the way they do in hockey.

I can give you one recent example from Kraft General Foods: the development of our fat-free products. Engineers played a key role in the development, not only of the processes that were fundamental to the product but also of the products themselves.

I can't overemphasize the importance of engineers like yourselves being team members with people from other disciplines. In any industry or organization, cross-functional teamwork is the mark of the innovative organization.

It's up to both the organization and the individual to make teamwork . . . work. The company has to see the importance of crossing the walls that naturally form between functions; it has to emphasize and promote teamwork.

But you as individuals have a role in it, too. Your colleagues in other disciplines may not share your technical vocabulary or even your view of the world—but you'll need to work with them, on projects to which each of you has a significant contribution to make.

When we developed our fat-free lines, product engineers worked with marketing people, with finance experts, with plant and operations people. It really was a basketball-team effort that got these innovative products to the marketplace so quickly.

To organize for innovation, we also have to[28] stay as close as possible to our customers . . . because that's how we know which of our inventions has the potential to become a real—that is to say, a useful, marketable—innovation. And we have to keep our technology base strong, through a long-range commitment to science and engineering programs.

Cross-functional teamwork . . . a fast-breaking basketball style of execution . . . an understanding of the consumer . . . and leading-edge technology: those are our four principles of innovation at Kraft General Foods.[29]

Other companies organize for innovation in their own ways. 3M has an excellent record, based on a few simple principles: they keep their divisions small (in fact, each division manager must know every staffer's first name) . . . they encourage experimentation and tolerate failure (each division's goal is to get 25 percent of its sales from products developed in the past five years) . . . they share internally developed technology throughout the company . . . and their researchers, marketers, and managers work with customers to brainstorm new product ideas.

Hewlett-Packard urges its researchers to spend 10 percent of their time on pet projects—and gives them 24-hour access to labs and equipment. Merck also gives its researchers time and resources to pursue high-risk, high-payoff projects.

My point is that there are lots of possibilities. And if you're in a company that consistently does any or all of the things I've mentioned . . . then you're in a place that's organized for innovation.[30]

Now let's narrow the focus still further.[31] Let's talk about you. Let's talk about innovation at the personal level . . . because when you get right down to it, it's not societies or organizations that innovate; it's people. So what can you, as an individual, do to train yourself to be an innovator?

First, I would advise you to **cultivate breadth.** Be a first-rate specialist—but be a generalist as well. Be like a doctor who's an excellent surgeon, but who also has the broad knowledge of a general practitioner. Of course, there is no substitute for strong functional expertise. But it's possible for engineers to become so functionally narrow that they don't have the capability for innovation. They may be great inventors—but poor innovators, just because they are so narrow.

So . . . even as knowledge increases exponentially, the key is to develop deep functional skills in your discipline (or sub-discipline) while you maintain a broad view of the world about you. To me, that's critical to the process of innovation—and to the progress that follows.[32]

Why?[33] Because in the world outside the university, the application of knowledge is far less compartmentalized than the acquisition of it. Finding an innovative solution to a problem may require you to employ concepts and insights from two or three or more different fields.

Time and again, innovation has come from crossing from one discipline to another . . . or from making a linkage between one branch of science or technology to another. In fact, the computer journalist Peter Borden, quoted in Roger van Oesch's 1983 book *A Whack on the Side of the Head*,[34] says that "most advances in science come when a person, for one reason or another, is forced to change fields."

You could even argue that this is the only way that innovation takes place.[35] Thomas Kuhn was the man who first described how and why it happens that from time to time, scientists in one field or another adopt whole new paradigms, whole new sets of assumptions and ways of looking at things.[36] And Kuhn said this:

> Under normal conditions the research scientist is not an innovator but a solver of puzzles, and the puzzles upon which he concentrates are just those which he believes can be both stated and solved within the existing scientific tradition.

In other words, the normal path to professional success encourages, even forces, specialization. But nevertheless, the true innovator resists it.

So what can you do? Well, I would say that it's up to you, both during your formal education and afterward, to perform the synthesis—to look for ways in which the various disciplines complement and reinforce each other . . . to learn, as early as possible, to think in terms of systems, to find the "networks," the "connective tissue" between one discipline and another.

And it's not only jumping from one branch of a discipline to another . . . or from one science to another . . . that helps you to grow into an innovator. It's a broad perspective on the world.[37]

The problem is that too many engineers are happy to live within the confines of their little world of engineering . . . as opposed to knowing what's happening in Iraq, or up in space, or in a film, play, or novel that has nothing to do with engineering. Carl Ally, founder of an advertising agency, once said that

> the creative person wants to be a know-it-all. He wants to know about all kinds of things: ancient history, nineteenth century mathematics, current manufacturing techniques, flower arranging, and hog futures. Because he never knows when these ideas might come together to form a new idea. It may happen six minutes later or six months or six years down the road. But he has faith that it will happen.

It's impossible to say, right now, just what combination of stimuli and inputs will catalyze your individual personality and intellect and produce innovation . . . which is why it's so important for you to make the range of inputs as wide as possible: reading *Dune*, or *Time*, or the *Atlantic* . . . or listening to jazz or minimalist music . . . or playing tennis on Saturday afternoon. What's tennis have to do with innovation? Maybe nothing.[38] Maybe it just frees up your mind for a while. Or maybe it gets you thinking about the infinity of possibilities within the simple, never-changing geometry of the court . . . or whatever.

Thirty years ago, I wondered why they made me take English composition and English literature. Now I know why. And I wish I'd had more, rather than less, of them. The composition improved my communication skills, which I'll come to in a moment, and the literature introduced me to other people—to their lives, their values, their personalities, their interactions with the world around them—all of which are key considerations for the engineers who would be innovators.[39]

Even the engineers who will go down in the annals of engineering as the world's best . . . were not narrowly focused. Maybe that mysterious "X factor" that defines the real innovator . . . came in some way from their other interests.

Examples? Well, the one I like is Antoine Lavoisier. He's best-known as the founder of modern chemistry. But he also pioneered in physiology, scientific agriculture, and technology . . . and was <u>also</u>, in his time, a leading figure in finance, economics, public education, and government. Makes you wonder when he had time to sleep![40]

Of course, back in the 18th century, it was easier to know a lot about everything than today, when our knowledge is doubling every 10 to 15 years. But that doesn't mean we shouldn't try. In our time, we have innovative geniuses like Edison, a man of very broad interests, or Buckminster Fuller, who was into architecture, automotive design, city planning, education, and even the technological perfection of humanity—and that's only a partial list of his interests.

Lavoisier, Edison, Fuller, and dozens of others weren't just engineers. They weren't holed up in their pilot plants or their labs. They had other interests. They were out doing other things with their lives.[41] And I hope you'll do the same.[42]

Along with functional expertise and breadth, I would advise you to **develop three separate but mutu-**

ally reinforcing sets of skills: analysis/problem solving, persuasion, and vision.

You don't have to worry too much about analysis and problem solving, because this is where American education excels. The training of engineers, accountants, financial people, systems analysts, and so on, all gears people for organizing, analyzing, and processing data; for finding solutions to problems; and for making decisions.

So to develop yourself in this area, you simply need to acquire a solid technical background in the basic disciplines and analytic techniques. The better your foundation, the better you'll be able to solve problems under an ever-changing variety of conditions and an onslaught of new information.

The second major skill area is **persuasion.**[43]

Back in 1865, Gregor Mendel made momentous discoveries in genetics—discoveries that had no effect for 35 years. That's partly because 19th-century anatomy and physiology didn't allow for the concept of discrete hereditary units; also, Mendel's statistical methodology was completely foreign to the biologists of his time. But that 35-year time lag may also have had something to do with the fact that Mendel was a modest monk living off the beaten path in a monastery in Moravia.

Or consider Oswald Avery, who made the milestone discovery that DNA was indeed the genetic material—in 1944, 21 years before Watson and Crick discerned its exact structure and function. Why wasn't his contribution recognized at the time?[44] Well, an article in the *Scientific American* points to his "quiet, self-effacing, non-disputatious" personality. Not exactly your high-powered Lee Iacocca type.[45]

But if you're going to be an innovator, you need a little of Lee Iacocca in you. Every innovator will encounter resistance, so every innovator needs to be able to sell his or her ideas—to influence, charm, persuade, arm-twist, compromise—do whatever it takes to get people to give his or her[46] ideas a fair hearing.

What can you do to become better in this area? Put strong emphasis on your interpersonal and communications skills. Make sure you take some courses in language, rhetoric, writing, human behavior, or speech communications. And get involved in group activities, clubs, or organizations; put yourself in settings in which you have a chance to persuade people to put ideas into action.[47]

Finally, to train yourself for innovation,[48] you need to **develop your imagination, your intuition, your vision.** You've got to be a little like the entrepreneurs, the dreamers, the visionaries, the "ship captains" who know their destination even though no one can see it.[49] These are people with a strong sense of purpose . . . and powerful beliefs about the way things should happen.

In business, they're people like Tom Watson, who founded IBM . . . like Alfred Sloan, who created the framework for the modern General Motors . . . like Henry Ford, who stated his vision very explicitly: "I will build a motor car for the great multitude . . . so low in price that no [one][50] will be unable to own one—and enjoy with his family the blessing of pleasure in God's great open spaces."

What can you do to become more of a visionary? Well, unfortunately, this ability is very hard to teach, and it isn't given much attention in school. The best way to get next to it is to expose yourself to examples: read biographies of successful visionaries in politics, business, and the arts; take courses in religious studies, philosophy, art history, and literature.

Now, I know that my comparing scientific innovators with poets and artists may seem far-fetched,[51] but it really isn't at all: both spend a lot of time in the world of the imagination, and both envision completely new arrangements of things. The leap to a new way of hearing or seeing, which artistic innovators make . . . really[52] isn't so different from the scientific innovator's leap to a new way of thinking.

Well, I've covered a lot of ground tonight, so let me sum it up for you:[53] Innovation is not the same as invention. Although we need both, it's innovation—the development of practical products and processes—that really drives economic growth and human progress. But neither progress nor innovation is guaranteed. That's why it's important that our societies promote innovation . . . that our companies organize for it . . . and that we as individuals—and you, as leaders of the future—train for it.[54]

I hope it's clear, from all I've said tonight, that although no single field has a monopoly on innovation, the engineering mind and the engineering discipline are well suited to the generation of innovative ideas.[55] I think Isaac Asimov[56] said it best: "Science can amuse and fascinate us all—but it is engineering that changes the world."

You have an opportunity to change the world.[57] I urge you to make the most of it.

NOTES

1. The speaker begins by establishing the relevance of his assigned topic—"progress and innovation"—to the audience's status as "leaders of the future."

2. The sentence establishes the rationale for what follows, as well as the speaker's purpose ("I'm going to help prepare you for your role"). It also lays out the structure of the speech: a Definition (what it is), followed by a Judgment (why we need it), a Consequence (what causes it), followed by another Consequence (actions—on the part of the audience—that will result in innovation).

3. This sentence introduces a definition of *innovation* (actually, as it turns out, a distinction—between *invention* and *innovation*). The term is defined by an anecdote (from Clifton Fadiman's book) which exemplifies it. Of course, I could have gone directly to the Drucker quotes, but the anecdote adds a storytelling element, and people love stories. It also makes the definition come alive. And it reflects well on women.

4. Note how carefully the anecdote is set up (mainly because the audience will probably have no idea who von Baeyer was)—two full sentences of background before the actual sequence of events begins.

5. No identification required for Peter Drucker. The venerable management scholar and consultant would be familiar to this audience.
6. This paragraph is an illustration of the way an idea can be developed by example.
7. Note the conversational language, with indefinite *you*.
8. Concept illustrated by example.
9. Creating coherence via repetition of the topic under discussion, i.e., the discontinuity of invention and innovation.
10. A mini-summary, in which the speaker seems to "take a breath" intellectually before plunging on to the next major idea.
11. Note how the quote is set up, with source identified.
12. The rhetorical question is appropriate after a provocative statement; the speaker appears to be reflecting the question that's in his listeners' minds.
13. An example of effective closure: these three concepts are arranged in the order in which they typically occur in real life.
14. Notice how thoroughly a key point is developed in this paragraph: (1) statement, (2) repetition (this is "complementary repetition"—the "everything else . . . " part repeats by filling in what the original statement does not say), (3) example, (4) repetition plus more information.
15. Again, note how this important point is developed in this and the preceding paragraphs. First the general point: "I'm not just talking about . . ." Then the examples. Then the reiteration, clearly marked with "My point is . . ." Then another repetition, slightly elaborated, to drive the point home.
16. This sentence establishes the relevance of the subject matter to the audience.
17. Topic-to-topic signpost: recaps what has been said, gives listeners a summary of the content of the rest of the speech.
18. Still more guidance for the listeners, telling them what to expect. Always remember to give your audience plenty of help in following the structure of the speech.
19. Note the personal style; impersonal would have been ". . . to which no one has the answer."
20. Note the conversational, colloquial style (as opposed to, e.g., "When all factors co-occur, the result can be impressive").
21. From my general reading, I knew that these ideas were not in the public domain, so the speaker could not have them in his knowledge base. In this situation, intellectual honesty requires that you attribute your material to the correct source.
22. Note rhythm: short sentences for abrupt events.
23. Same point as in Note 22.
24. The whole paragraph is a signpost. Again, the speaker summarizes what he's said and prepares the audience for what comes next.

25. Again, a very careful and elaborate set-up: first, the idea of "a comparison" is introduced; then come the terms of the comparison (basketball versus football); then the elaboration (why modern management is more like basketball).

26. Note the inter-sentence signpost that expresses the relationship between the two sentences.

27. Note the paragraph-to-paragraph transition. These two examples could have been linked with a simple *also*, but the word would have gone by so fast that the audience might have missed the connection between the two points (i.e., that both are ways of organizing for innovation). I can't overemphasize the importance of patiently walking your audience through the highways and byways of your speech structure.

28. Repetition of the topic under consideration helps keep the audience on track.

29. Note the "here's-what-I've-told-you" summary before moving to the other companies.

30. Establishing relevance of subject matter to audience: the information about innovative companies isn't just academic knowledge—it can help the listeners with their career planning.

31. Note the signpost and its contemporary-sounding video imagery. Also note the highly personal style, appropriate for those times in your speech when you are directly addressing your audience: "Let's talk about you."

32. Notice how I consistently tie the point under consideration back to the main theme of the speech.

33. The *Why?* adds a note of interactivity, of audience involvement, as if the speaker is saying, "'Why?' you ask."

34. Again, the quote is set up carefully, in proportion to the obscurity of the person quoted. Giving the title of the book that the quote came from is generally not required, but here I thought it added to the credibility of the quote.

35. This sentence is actually a lead-in to the quote; it prepares the audience for the quote by "pre-stating" it in one-level-up terms.

36. Here the reason for the elaborate set-up is not so much the author's obscurity (many in an audience of engineering students might know who he is), but the importance of his groundbreaking insight.

37. Note the two-sentence intersection signpost.

38. Again, note the use of rhetorical questions to create a sense of dialogue with the audience.

39. An example of convincing the audience via personal experience.

40. The speaker not only anticipates the audience's reaction to his material—he gives his own reaction to it. This is another technique for making speeches sound less like a book being read and more like a live person talking.

41. Again, note the technique for repeating key points. And notice how the structure of the sentences—they're all short, they all begin with *They*—reinforces the repetition.

42. Establishing relevance to the audience (so that they are never left thinking, "Why is he telling me this?").

43. Note signpost.

44. See note 33.

45. See note 40.

46. Note use of double pronoun to avoid sexist phraseology.

47. Here the speaker's suggestions are reinforced through repetitive sentence structure—three consecutive sentences phrased as (polite) commands.

48. Note the signpost that conveys the idea of "last in a series" and repeats the topic under consideration.

49. Being a visionary is a somewhat novel idea for an engineering student, so a little repetition is appropriate: three words that exemplify the desired qualities, plus a metaphor (a "semi-metaphor," actually, because neither metaphoric mariners—the entrepreneurs—nor real ones can see their destinations).

50. I edited the quote—Henry actually said "no man." I know—I told you not to do that, but this was a very subtle change to a really great quote. "No man" would have detracted from its impact. It was a judgment call.

51. Another example of making the speech interactive by anticipating the audience's reaction to the material.

52. Note push-word, with its subtle message: "This is how things are."

53. Signpost that prepares audience for the summary to come.

54. Summarizing the speech by recapping its content.

55. Close by relating the subject matter to the audience.

56. Isaac Asimov is another writer who needs no introduction to this audience.

57. An example of a "coda" (or "exit comment") that repeats part of the quote. The coda leads into a third closing strategy (the first: summary; the second: audience relevance): vision—what the speaker hopes will happen.

Summary

How to Make Your Speeches Cogent and Memorable

Here I want to present a "summary-plus" that covers everything I've explained, as well as a few other points I consider relevant to the writing of cogent and memorable speeches.

Why these two criteria, out of all the adjectives that might describe what we're trying for?

The answer comes out of my experience. A couple of years ago, an executive client, in our preliminary interview, gave me those two key words as goals for the two speeches we were going to write. Of course: we wanted the speeches to impress the audience and be recalled long after the event itself. That one comment, from the mouth of a client, summarized the goals of rhetoric.

This vice president was going to give the opening and closing remarks at a day-long meeting of his top 120 people—his direct reports and their staffs.

He's a relaxed, affable, very intelligent guy with a good sense of humor. However, most of his public speaking consists of budget reviews. How would we get to "cogent and memorable"?

Well, as the Italian politician and statesman Vittorio Emanuele Orlando once observed, "Oratory is like prostitution. You have to have little tricks."

I decided that I needed a full arsenal, especially since the occasion was hardly dripping with drama.

That's a key point: a lot of cogent and memorable speeches aren't especially challenging to write. They're what I call slam-dunks: the context—a Civil War battlefield, a crying social need, a space shuttle explosion, a nation under attack from the skies, an economic crisis—is itself so cogent and memorable that the speechwriter has no trouble driving right to the heart of the matter.

Of course, that's not to say that all Gettysburg Addresses are created equal. Lincoln executed his much better than Whatzisname, who spoke for two hours. But in both cases, context and situation were powerful components of "cogent and memorable."

That was not the case here, so I cast my intellectual net as wide as possible. I thought about all the speeches I'd written, read, and heard. I wanted to include not only "internalities"—matters of structure and content—but also "externalities" such as the speaker's behavior, the audience's involvement, and the speaker-audience dynamics.

Here's the list I came up with:

■ Strong theme/story line (preferably with suspense).

Ken Askew, an outstanding speechwriter, made me aware of the importance of this one. He's a literature major, whereas my field is linguistics. Ken himself once gave a speech that very eloquently spelled out the significance of story, of tension and resolution, of problem and solution, of an ending that somehow completes the beginning.

■ Clear moral/bottom line.

It's the last thing they hear, so if you can make it the best thing they hear, you're well on the way toward "cogent and memorable." What does your conclusion mean for your listeners and their lives? What general principle is confirmed (or refuted)?

■ Powerful, intense rhetoric that speaks of a serious problem or dire consequences, or that conveys vehement advocacy or a lofty vision.

Powerful rhetoric gets people's attention, so use it sparingly. Most corporate rhetoric is so low in intensity that a little goes a long way. On the other hand, most political campaign rhetoric is so overheated that it loses credibility.

■ Simple "why-didn't-I-think-of-that?" solution/ argument.

Perhaps you can unify items that have until now seemed disparate—or bring together ideas that seem irreconcilable. You might show how one solution, already doable, is applicable to the current problem, or that the unfamiliar is really familiar, thus less threatening—or even to be welcomed. Or maybe you can justify something via a principle the audience already believes in.

In any case, you create a quick, easy—but heretofore unseen—path to a desirable goal.

■ Personal testimony/experience/anecdotes.

We all know how audiences love stories. But there's another reason for personal testimony: authenticity. When a speaker speaks from experience, no one can question the truth of what he or she is saying.

This came home to me vividly in working with my executive client. He wanted to congratulate his people on being first-rate professionals in their field. I asked him to authenticate the qualities he was praising them for, through his own experience—and he did. The very qualities that had gotten his people through an extraordinarily difficult year had gotten him through some difficult career setbacks. Somehow, I don't think it was a coincidence.

■ Effective use of ornamental material—quotes, humor, statistics, historical references.

This one pretty much speaks for itself. The conventional advice is "less is more" and "know your audience," and I agree. Again, authenticity is important; it's so easy to sound fake with this stuff. Don't use material just because it seems clever or impressive. Make sure it reinforces—and doesn't distract from—your main theme.

Really effective speech humor comes not from long narrative jokes with guffaw-producing punch lines (they rarely work, partly because most of us don't have the talent to tell them, partly because the really funny ones are R-rated or otherwise inappropriate), but from wry, chuckle-producing one-liners and asides that come out of your wit and the speech situation. For example,

> To begin with, the segmentation of media continues, **as we move toward the day when each one of us will have his or her own magazine and cable channel.**
> As that happens, the "traditional" advertising venues continue to explode. Today we have six networks, versus the three that we had only ten years ago. **For those of us with too much time on our hands**, there are 22 daytime talk shows . . . 89 national and cable networks (versus 29 only 10 years ago) . . . and thousands of magazine titles.[1]

■ Summarizing via slogans, acronyms,[2] and aphorisms (or "sound bites," as they're called today)—especially at the end.

We can't all rhyme like Jesse Jackson or Johnny Cochran—nor should we try. But a well-constructed acronym or aphorism can be a powerful mnemonic device. You just have to be careful not to clutter up the overall message with a lot of other clever devices.

I confess, I've never been able to write sound bites by setting out to do so. I try to summarize major points with appropriate generalities and to say everything in a rhythmic, balanced way, and the better examples may acquire sound-bite status.

Maybe you're able to crank 'em out at will. Maybe you're the kind of person Thomas Fuller had in mind when he observed, back in 1731, that "constant popping off of proverbs will make thee a byword thyself." If so, you have my admiration.

■ Key "grabber" metaphor or analogy.

These tend to come in flashes of insight, after you've got your whole speech in mind and can imagine what your main theme is similar to. Here's an example:

A couple of weeks ago, I was driving my car through what you might call a war zone. But I wasn't worried about my safety, because this was only a supermarket war zone.

Actually it was a suburb north of Chicago, where, in addition to the usual take-out and fast-food outlets, there's a local grocery chain, called Sunset Foods, which competes very successfully with more conventional supermarkets because it employs small armies of people

who are always ready to unload your cart at the checkout counter, then load your bags into your car when
you pull up.

You would think that Sunset had a lock on the
extra-service segment, especially since they recently
remodeled and expanded, but now Minneapolis-based
Byerly's is about to set up shop in the same suburb,
and their store will offer all of the above, plus it will
be open 24 hours a day.

Meanwhile, the local Dominick's—a large Chicago-
based chain—has added a whole "fresh store" with
fresh-baked breads, produce, and so forth.

The local Jewel store—Dominick's' archrival—is
Siamese twins with an Osco drug store; there's no
physical boundary between the two, and you can use
checkout counters at either one.

And just across the border, in the next suburb,
another chain, called Fresh Fields, with emphasis on
the organic and natural, is about to open.

All of these stores are within five minutes' drive of
each other.

Yes, it's a war out there. Traditional grocery stores
are battling each other, as well as take-out restaurants
like Boston Market . . . and new competitors like
Whole Foods and PeaPod. It's a battle for share of
stomach—for share of total food consumed, at home
or away from home.

This battle is the central issue that our industry
faces, and today I'm going to talk about winning—by
focusing on the consumer. As we take ECR from vision
to reality, we must focus it even more on benefits to
consumers, so that we bring them into grocery stores
more often—and serve them better once they're there.

So there's the message in a nutshell. As I spell it all
out in more detail, I'll talk about some of the challenges that we at Kraft Foods have faced—and the
lessons we've learned—as we've tried to turn the ECR
vision into reality. I hope all of that will be useful to
those companies who are not yet fully engaged.[3]

I'm not that creative in the metaphor department either. The effectiveness of the above example comes not from the freshness of the metaphor ("business as battle" is hardly new) but from the way the image catches the audience off guard and from the contrast between supermarkets and combat.

I am pretty good at puns, so I tend to start with metaphors that already exist, then build on them with related ideas.

In one of my own speeches, I started by talking about the "political landscape," then went into the "fault lines" of the landscape, then into the "bed of sand" underneath.

You can also use idea-generating software like Ideafisher to generate associations that you can convert into analogies and metaphors.

■ Audience involvement.

Audiences are normally so passive during speeches that a little involvement can help make the speech memorable, simply because afterwards, people can "anchor" the speech-event, in their memories, to something that they actually did during the speech.

You can single out individuals or groups for recognition (as the executive did during his speech).

You can use props or physical devices such as a voice vote, a show of hands, or applause (which the executive also did, applauding his people and urging them to applaud themselves).

There are two other forms of audience involvement that are internal to the speech: a compelling "what's-in-it-for-me?" bottom line and a clear "I-know-where-you're-coming-from" message. These tap into two of the most powerful sources of interpersonal bonding—empathy and benefit.

■ Polished delivery with appropriate gestures and emotions.

That's really a no-brainer. I included it just for completeness, although for us ghostwriters, it's often a real challenge to convince our clients that it really matters.

So there you have the ingredients. Not all of them will work for every speech. But the more of them you use (and I emphasize: use appropriately) the more cogent and memorable your speeches will be.

NOTES

1. "The Internet Is the Answer—But What Is the Question?" Keynote remarks by Kathy Olvany Riordan, Director, Media Services, Kraft Foods, at the Ad Club of New York's "Best Interactive Agencies of 1996" Program, New York, NY, Dec. 18, 1996.

2. For example, communications consultant Jack Pyle structures his presentations on public speaking around the acronym SPEAK: Smile, Posture, Eye contact, Animation, Kinetics (gestures). Copyrighted material used with permission.

3. "ECR: From Vision to Reality." Keynote address by John Bowlin, President, Kraft Foods, at the general session of the annual Efficient Consumer Response (ECR) Conference, Chicago, IL, Mar. 15, 1996.

EPILOGUE

A Few Last Words: Speechmaking as Behavior—and Why the Principles of Good Speechwriting Are What They Are

As I said earlier, you can't just stop when your message is complete. There has to be a little leave-taking ritual. That's the purpose of these last few words.

I want to put everything I've said into a larger context by addressing the basic question that always occurs to us whenever we're told to do something in a certain way: "Why?" Why are the principles of good communication the ones I've given you here, as opposed to any others you might have been taught—or indeed, any others that there could be?

The answer is that speechmaking is a form of behavior, so the characteristics of good speeches are just particular versions of the principles of good behavior:

■ **Purpose and selection.** A good speech is clear about its purpose. It contains only material that is relevant to the writer's goals and the audience's needs—and nothing more.

Similarly, in everyday life, we should not be devious about our motives; nor should we belabor or mislead people with extraneous words or actions.

■ **Arrangement; coherence and listenability; economy.** Good speeches arrange their subject matter in a reasonable order that reflects the speaker's thought processes, and the nature of the arrangement is clear from the signals that he/she provides.

A good speech is clear and coherent. It is free of ambiguity. The audience can easily—effortlessly, in fact—interpret its sentences and discern the relationship between one piece and the next and between each piece and the whole. All of the audience's attention and mental energy are thus saved for the message itself.

A good speech is economical: it makes optimal use of the resources of the language; it never repeats without a purpose; and it uses no more words than are necessary to fulfill the writer's aims and the audience's needs.

By the same token, in everyday life, we should refrain from making unnecessary or inappropriate demands on the time and attention of other people.

■ **Appropriateness of style and word choice.** Good speechwriting selects those items of vocabulary and those grammatical forms that are appropriate to the audience's sensibilities, the writer's purpose, and the type and topic of communication.

And in life, we should try, to the extent possible, to make other people comfortable by accommodating ourselves to their expectations and preferences.

So really, good speechwriting is consistent with good living. And I hope you'll do plenty of both.

About Toastmasters International

If the thought of public speaking is enough to stop you dead in your tracks, it may have the same effect on your career.

While surveys report that public speaking is one of people's most dreaded fears, the fact remains that the inability to effectively deliver a clear thought in front of others can spell doom for professional progress. The person with strong communication skills has a clear advantage over tongue-tied colleagues—especially in a competitive job market.

Toastmasters International, a nonprofit educational organization, helps people conquer their pre-speech jitters. From one club started in Santa Ana, California, in 1924, the organization now has more than 170,000 members in 8,300 clubs in 62 countries.

How Does It Work?

A Toastmasters club is a "learn by doing" workshop in which men and women hone their communication and leadership skills in a friendly, supportive atmosphere. A typical club has 20 members who meet weekly or biweekly to practice public speaking techniques. Members, who pay approximately $35 in dues twice a year, learn by progressing through a series of 10 speaking assignments and being evaluated on their performance by their fellow club members. When finished with the basic speech manual, members can select from among 14 advanced programs that are geared toward specific career needs. Members also have the opportunity to develop and practice leadership skills by working in the High Performance Leadership Program.

Besides taking turns to deliver prepared speeches and evaluate those of other members, Toastmasters give impromptu talks on assigned topics, usually related to current events. They also develop listening skills, conduct meetings, learn parliamentary procedure and gain leadership experience by serving as club officers. But most importantly, they develop self-confidence from accomplishing what many once thought impossible.

The benefits of Toastmasters' proven and simple learning formula has not been lost on the thousands of corporations that sponsor in-house Toastmasters clubs as cost-efficient means of satisfying their employees' needs for communication training. Toastmasters clubs can be found in the U.S. Senate and the House of Representatives, as well as in a variety of community organizations, prisons, universities, hospitals, military bases, and churches.

How to Get Started

Most cities in North America have several Toastmasters clubs that meet at different times and locations during the week. If you are interested in forming or joining a club, call (714) 858-8255. For a listing of local clubs, call (800) WE-SPEAK, or write Toastmasters International, PO Box 9052, Mission Viejo, California 92690, USA. You can also visit our website at http://www.toastmasters.org.

As the leading organization devoted to teaching public speaking skills, we are devoted to helping you become more effective in your career and daily life.

Terrence J. McCann
Executive Director, Toastmasters International

About the National Speaker's Association

The National Speakers Association (NSA) is an international association of more than 3,700 members dedicated to advancing the art and value of experts who speak professionally. Specific purposes of NSA are:

- Defining and supporting standards of excellence in professional speaking;
- Enhancing the communication competencies and business skills of professional speakers;
- Promoting the value of professional speakers as effective sources of expertise, knowledge and insight; and
- Expanding the marketplace for professional speaking.

NSA delivers a multifaceted environment for advancing the careers of professional speakers. Virtually all of NSA's programs, meetings, publications and resources are structured around eight professional competencies. Together, they are designed to give organization and substance to the educational and professional advancement of each member. The professional competencies are: Authorship and Product Development; Managing the Business; Platform Mechanics; Presenting and Performing; Professional Awareness; Professional Relationships; Sales and Marketing; and Topic Development.

The programming for NSA's Educational Workshops, Annual Conventions and single-focus Learning Labs are based on these competencies. While a minimum number of paid presentations must be documented to qualify a speaker for membership in NSA, nonmembers are welcome to attend chapter and national meetings and can subscribe to *Professional Speaker* magazine.

For more information, contact the National Speakers Association, 1500 S. Priest Drive, Tempe, Arizona 85281; Phone: 602-968-2552; Fax: 602-968-0911; E-mail: nsamain@aol.com; Web Site: http://www.nsa speaker.org.

Allyn & Bacon presents...

The **Essence of Public Speaking** Series

Endorsed by Toastmasters International and the National Speakers Association

"These excellent books are ideal for [those] who want to offer practical ideas about the wonderful world of paid speaking... and are also ideal for those who want to speak to promote their professions, careers, or causes. *The Essence of Public Speaking* books are easy to understand, and simple to activate."

— Dottie Walters, President, Walters International Speakers Bureau, Publisher, *Sharing Ideas Magazine for Speakers*, and Author of *Speak & Grow Rich*

Speaking for Profit and Pleasure: Making the Platform Work for You,
by William D. Thompson

"If you want to skyrocket your career as a platform professional this is your guide to absolute success. A practical, step-by-step plan for marketing yourself — and for creating your own powerful niche in the world of speaking."

— Glenna Salsbury, CSP, CPAE, Author of *The Art of The Fresh Start*

Speaking Your Way to the Top: Making Powerful Business Presentations,
by Marjorie Brody

"[This] is a comprehensive, well-written guide for anyone who needs to know how to present themselves effectively in today's marketplace. I highly recommend it!"

— Tony Alessandra, Ph.D., CSP, CPAE, Co-author of *The Platinum Rule*

TechEdge: Using Computers to Present and Persuade, by William J. Ringle

"A completely thorough guide to using current technology to support your presenting and consulting business. I would consider this the definitive guide to using computers as a speaker."

— Hal Slater, DTM, Toastmasters International Accredited Speaker and Author of *First Call Closing* and *Managing and Motivating Salespeople*

Using Stories and Humor—Grab Your Audience,
by Joanna Campbell Slan

"This book is more than another how-to guide on public speaking. It is a rare find! It will allow you to see your experiences as a rich and abundant resource of humor and stories. It will surely enhance your speaking but it will also enrich your life. It's brilliant!"

— Morgan McArthur, ATM, Toastmasters International 1994 World Champion of Public Speaking

Writing Great Speeches: Professional Techniques You Can Use,
by Alan Perlman

"If you have ever asked the question 'How do I write a winning speech?', Alan Perlman has the answer. This book is a must-read for professional and amateurs alike."

— Mark Brown, ATM, Toastmasters International 1995 World Champion of Public Speaking